PROTESTANT
CHURCH MUSIC
IN
AMERICA

BY
ARCHIBALD T. DAVISON
Ph. D., F. R. C. M., Mus. D.

E. C. SCHIRMER MUSIC CO.
BOSTON   MASS.

First printing 1933
Second printing 1936

E. C. S. No. 809

To
EDWARD CALDWELL MOORE
CHAIRMAN OF THE BOARD OF PREACHERS OF
HARVARD UNIVERSITY, EMERITUS

WHOSE SYMPATHETIC COÖPERATION AND UNFAILING
INSIGHT MADE POSSIBLE EIGHTEEN YEARS OF
IDEAL RELATIONSHIP BETWEEN CLERGYMAN AND
CHOIR-MASTER.

PREFACE

For those who are seeking a history of Protestant church music in America this book will have but little interest. To trace the swing of the pendulum from Puritan insistence on the plainer forms of church music to the modern acceptance of music of almost every type as material worthy to have a part in religious exercise is the historian's task. This volume makes no such scholarly pretense. It aims, rather, to point out attitudes and conditions which now govern our church music; to make clear certain powers and limitations of music in general which specifically apply to the present problem; to define, through technical analysis, the main features of sacred as opposed to secular style; to propose an ideal of Protestant church music; and finally, to state what means and material are suitable for the realization of that ideal. Such suggestions as are here made relative to church music administration and procedure are entirely practical; they are not predicated upon conditions which are rarely found and then only in the perfect church; their active adoption is easily within the reach of all.

A part of the material to be found in these pages is drawn from articles and lectures on church music prepared by the author: notably from three addresses, one delivered before the Unitarian Laymen's League in 1919; the second at the Princeton Theological School in 1924, and subsequently published in the Methodist Review of May-June, 1925; the third before the American Guild of Organists in 1932.

The author wishes to thank the following firms for permission to reproduce brief excerpts from their publications: G. Schirmer, Inc., The Boston Music Company, Oliver Ditson Company, Inc., The H. W. Gray Company, Novello & Co., The Oxford University Press, Hawkes & Son, and J. Curwen & Sons. Grateful acknowledgment is also made to Mr. Mason Hammond for valuable advice; and, in particular, to Mr. Edward B. Gammons for varied and extensive assistance.

ARCHIBALD THOMPSON DAVISON

Harvard University, 1933

CONTENTS

PROTESTANT CHURCH MUSIC IN AMERICA

PART I

ATTITUDES AND CONDITIONS AFFECTING PROTESTANT CHURCH MUSIC

General Considerations

It is doubtful whether there is any widespread dissatisfaction with the music of the Protestant church in America. Articles on church music appear from time to time in musical magazines and church papers; clubs and forums give attention when some lecturer presents a talk upon "Hymns, New and Old, with their Stories," or upon "Choir Boys who have become Famous." Occasionally, to be sure, there is an outbreak against the existing forms and practices of church music; there may even be talk of a drastic reform; but from all the verbal and literary treadmill of denunciation only incidental and temporary benefits have ever issued. Martin Luther held a theory of Protestant church music which was fundamental, lofty, and at the same time practical. Yet in spite of the immediate need of a musical order suited to his new theology, in spite of a vision which embraced every aspect of the musical needs of the Reformed Church, and regardless of Luther's broadminded and energetic administration which scorned not to make use of any skill or any means to make his belief musically articulate, so powerful was the force of tradition that it was not, perhaps, until the eighteenth century that his ideal, in its most important particular at least, reached fulfillment. In this there is consolation for those of us who hold no reasonable expectation of immediate improvement.

Many musicians who live by a high professional standard refuse to associate themselves with the music of the church. They recognize that among the major branches of musical activity ecclesiastical music occupies the lowest station, and rather than exert themselves in a field which is traditionally unfriendly to idealism, they remain at a safe distance lest they be counted among the opprobrious company of 'church musicians.' It is no exaggeration to say that the better educated musician looks with suspicion upon any member of his profession who holds a church position, for he knows in practically every case that to be in the pay of a Protestant congregation means subscription to a situation which no musician of ideals could possibly tolerate. I have known several instances of courageous young musicians who have resigned their churches because to comply with the existing standards meant loss of self-respect and a sick conscience. For them, withdrawal was the only escape. Others, working under less hopeless circumstances, have persevered and in certain instances have accomplished much. To musicians like these who view church music as a principle rather than as a profession, its present state is indeed discouraging. They are jealous that in a house devoted to the worship of God no music shall be offered before Him which is not the best which it is humanly possible to offer.

It is indeed far too easy to visit wholesale condemnation upon a situation which is bad in many prominent features, and in the course of this book much will inevitably be said which implies deep dissatisfaction with church music as it is. On the other hand, we should hail with joy the fact that some churches, at least, are cultivating better music, better not necessarily in performance, but in material, and while fundamentally the situation cannot change until many things of which I shall later speak have come to pass, there is every reason to hope that more and more churches will undertake to improve the *quality* of their music.

In America we dislike to go in for reform in a small way. We want to abolish *all* of one particular evil, or we desire to improve an entire department of activity. Consequently we legislate, if we can, and failing that, we turn to organization on a large scale, forgetting that the important work of the world generally gets done by the few. No society for the improvement of church music is likely to accomplish much; at least, it never has. The good that has transpired has come from individuals largely endowed with *faith, courage, persistence,* and a *clear purpose.* These individuals working quietly, in a small way, and without the handicap of publicity, have given demonstrable proof of the superiority of a high standard over a low one. It is not through the shirkers or the discouraged or the indifferent that improvement will come, but by the efforts of those sincere and consecrated persons who realize that 'good' is better than 'poor' and that those who come after may achieve the 'best.'

Indifference

It is, I suppose, an inescapable trait of human nature that the indifference bred in us by custom and routine often ends by dulling our discrimination between the important and the trivial, the beautiful and the ugly, the good and the bad. And to this inevitable failing may justly be ascribed at least some of the evils which now beset the music of our churches. Sunday after Sunday, from childhood to old age, we hear the organ play its prelude and postlude; to its beguiling voice, often abetted by the choir, we lay our offering upon the collection plate, a trifle conscious, perhaps, that "give and it shall be given" was something more than rhetoric; we stand up for the hymn and we sit down when it is done; and we remain placid or are moved to irritation by the anthem, depending upon whether or not it pleases us. But from one year's end to the other, except as we receive some unaccustomed jolt to our routine-hardened sensibilities, we rarely even think about the real significance of our church music. The only mental perturbations we suffer over the music result in comment on its externals and then, in general, only if they displease us. We like or dislike the singing or the playing, but we do not question ourselves as to the appropriateness of the thing sung or played. We never attempt to formulate a theory of church music by which to test its quality. We never even ask ourselves whether the ends of worship would not be better served if music were completely banished from the service. We have always been accustomed to music in church and we would react to a service without music much as we would to a coffee-less breakfast.

All this is true, I say, until a startling situation arises which calls into question some detail in church music practice; but even then, such crises usually lead us to seek immediate and superficial reforms without driving us to fundamental inquiries. Some years ago an Episcopal church in the outskirts of Boston, desiring to achieve particular distinction in its Easter music, hired a member of the Boston Opera Company to sing at its morning service. I feel sure that the solo displayed the dramatic virtues of that particular singer's voice and that the text was, from a church point of view, unexceptionable; by which I mean that though the music may have been drawn from *Carmen* or *La Favorita* the canon of the church is very explicit in regard to what may be sung by way of text. At the conclusion of the solo the singer moved from the stalls to a position directly in front of the altar, where, turning his back squarely on the cross, he bowed three times in recognition of the applause with which at the moment the congregation could not, or at least did not, reward him.[1]

This is, admittedly, an unusual case, the result of a compound of causes with only one of which, namely indifference, I am at the moment dealing. Yet in perhaps a large majority of American Protestant churches there exists in some degree and kind the very same element of 'inappropriateness,' to term it gently, which in an extreme form appears in this fantastic narrative of the Easter canticle.

Complacency

Now I am sure that if American Protestant congregations were generally faced with the charge of entertaining unsuitable music in their churches they would challenge it vigorously. In exactly the tone of those embarrassed suburban worshippers inveighing against their choir-master's taste in permitting such an outrage against decency, the average church member would assert that under no circumstances could such a scandal befall in his own parish, at the same time pointing out the fact that the music there always

---

[1] Unity of form and a tradition for dignity usually prevent exhibitions of 'musical disorderly conduct' in the Episcopal service. None the less, individualistic tampering with the rubric is far too common. In one Episcopal church it is the invariable Easter custom to replace the *Gloria in Excelsis* by "The Lost Chord" played on the trumpet.

sounds reverent, and adding, perhaps, that there is no giggling in the choir and that all the singers are communicants. Yet it is quite likely that his church is equally culpable with regard to the inappropriateness of the music and the secular quality of the performance. The main difference lies in the fact that the representatives of one have been shocked at something which was the logical consummation of conditions to which they have thoughtlessly subscribed, while the others remain satisfied with a situation which has, as yet, presented no feature to which an unobservant congregation might take exception. When such a feature does appear, the net result of the ensuing agitation will be the discharge of some one or the taking of precautions to prevent a repetition of the embarrassing circumstance. Meanwhile, organists will continue to play the traditional preludes and postludes, choirs will go on singing their 'respectable' repertoires, the monthly musical services with their accompaniment of enlarged congregations and augmented collections will proceed as usual, and that is all there will be to it. No one will ask a fundamental question and put his answer to a searching test. No one will inquire into the ultimate purpose of church music, or as to exactly what hymns, organ music, and anthems, reduced to the cold terms of technical musical analysis, can and will carry out that purpose. No one will speculate as to the best kind of choir to make that music articulate in the sense of fulfilling the purpose for which the music was sung.   Congregations will remain content to accept their music as it is, either because they do not care or because they perceive no immediate reason for caring.

I wish at this point to be as specific as possible, because I am sure that the readers of this book have not yet discovered that I am including them in my company of the indifferent and the complacent.   Let me say at once then, that I would under no circumstances permit solo singing, even incidental to an anthem; and for the same reasons, multiplied by four, I would not tolerate a quartet, mixed, male, or female.   I consider as unsuited to the service such anthems as "The King of Love my Shepherd is," "Christian, the morn breaks sweetly o'er thee," and "Hark, hark, my soul" by Shelley; "Fierce was the wild billow," and "The souls of the righteous" by Noble; "King All Glorious," "Sweet is Thy mercy," and "The First Christmas" by Barnby; "Our Master hath a garden" by Crimp; "O for a closer walk with God" by Foster; "The voice in the wilderness" by Scott; "Open the gates of the temple" by Knapp; "Hail, gladdening Light" by Martin; "By Babylon's wave" by Gounod; "Brightest and best" by Parker; "Build thee more stately mansions" by Andrews; and "As torrents in summer" by Elgar, to name a few anthems frequently found upon the calendars even of metropolitan churches.   I consider as quite unworthy of congregational effort such hymn tunes as *Materna* ("O mother dear, Jerusalem"); *Penitence* ("In the hour of trial"); *St. Christopher* ("Beneath the Cross of Jesus"); *St. Cuthbert* ("Our blest Redeemer, ere He breathed"); *Margaret* ("O Love that will not let me go"); *St. Gertrude* ("Onward, Christian Soldiers"); *Ewing* ("Jerusalem the golden"); *Benediction* ("Saviour, again to Thy dear name we raise"); *Diademata* ("Crown Him with many crowns"); and all others of like musical calibre.[1]

I ask the reader to believe that in the foregoing I am not indulging in musical snobbism or highbrow affectation. My musical inclinations outside the church are thoroughly catholic. I proclaim my delight in jazz, Wagner, Gilbert and Sullivan, Hindemith, Jerome Kern, Schumann, and Johann Strauss, but I cannot conscientiously entertain any of these gentlemen within the doors of the church. This attitude does not arise from caprice or, primarily, from artistic consideration, but is justified by scientific and technical reasons with which I shall later deal in this book.

To refer for the last time to that unfortunate episode of Easter Day, I confess that save for a natural revulsion against such a gesture of sacrilege I cannot deplore the mountebank skipping through his vocal hoop before a Christian altar for the entertainment of an audience assembled to celebrate their Saviour's resurrection. Would that this, and even more, might

---

[1] A representative but by no means inclusive list of organ compositions, anthems, and hymns which seem to me to be worthy of acceptance will be found in the Appendix (List of Anthems, Hymns, and Organ Selections).

transpire in a thousand American churches if only by its sickening blasphemy to shake us out of our indifference and complacency and to force us to view our church music not as right merely because it is church music.

Isolation

Certain branches of musical activity tend to compartmentalize themselves to such an extent that they become isolated from the main current of the art. Adopting their own methods and standards and even their own vocabulary, they acquire a kind of ingrowing tradition that gathers about it prerogatives not considered valid in the larger field of music. Public school music, so-called, has been a notable example of this tendency; a kind of cloistered area of music education where only those conversant with the pedagogic patter of the school musician were on familiar ground, and where the timid objector who insisted that music even for children ought, after all, to be *real music* was countered with the grim interrogation, "But have you ever taught in Grade III?" While public school music, due largely to its failure to justify itself as preparation for the whole musical experience of life, is being gradually forced to conform to the procedures of the great world of music whose existence until recently it has very generally ignored, other fields of endeavor still insist upon their independence. Such is the men's chorus, popularly known as 'male' voices, though the ascription of sex to any voice becomes in this case doubly incomprehensible when upon examination of the music generally employed by these organizations one discovers only the most shadowy intimations of masculinity. Surely I need not develop the theme of the 'male voice mind;' it is the unique possession of the man who, as a rule, sings only in a men's chorus. Such a man will appreciatively attend a performance of the *B-minor Mass* or *The Messiah*, but will talk like a potential wifebeater when anyone suggests bringing in the ladies for a joint concert with him and his vocal associates; he will listen intently to *Die Meistersinger*, yet he will once a week blandly devote himself to the delights of musical adolescence at a rehearsal of the Orpheus Club.

Church music is still another example of a compartmentalized activity. During the golden period of its history, church music was great partly because it was the only music in the world subjected to critical review; it simply *had* to be great. But in our day, no one ever criticizes church music by the standards of other musical undertakings. Few of us would retain our posts if church services were reported by professional music critics and if people paid a set fee to hear us and our choirs. As we are not critized by *music* standards, but by *church music* standards, we become isolated in the same sense that men's choruses are isolated, and musical criticism treats us as it treats them, by passing by on the other side; and all too easily we, ourselves, come to the conclusion that there is, after all, little or nothing about us to criticize.   I would not wish to be understood as implying that church music should be judged as one would judge secular concert music or opera, for I firmly believe that the validity of church music depends upon the completeness with which it abjures all the personal and secular elements of concert performance, and upon its distance, both in style and substance, from the music of the world outside the church.   In the Middle Ages and in the sixteenth century, both the church and the world frankly borrowed from each other's resources to enrich their own particular body of music.   But at that time styles were not strongly divergent.   One musical language, with certain characteristic idioms suitable to one or the other, served both the church and the people. To-day, partly because of the immensely superior strength of the world and its associations, any attempt on the part of the church to use secular material or methods in its services merely ends in the secularization of worship.   Service music should be not one whit less good than the best secular music, but, like worship itself, the power and integrity of church music ought to be judged by the degree of its remoteness from the world.

Deficient Music Education

Three forces stand in virtual control of Protestant music: the minister, the church musician, and the layman.   Considering the importance of their charge all three are, from the point of view of musical training, sorely deficient.

The first question we ask concerning anyone even moderately educated in the arts is "How good is his taste?" Taste is not at all the same thing as instinct. One may enjoy performances of Beethoven and Bach and yet be possessed only of good musical instinct; but if one selects Beethoven and Bach over certain other composers for reasons which he clearly understands and which are based in the technique and the æsthetic of music, he may be said to have good musical taste. A man may enjoy Beethoven and Bach and react with equal satisfaction to Gounod or to Dubois, simply because his impression derives exclusively from the sense-impact made upon it by the music. Had he been taught to base his opinions on an intellectual weighing of the technical and æsthetic merits of the musical speech of these composers, in a comprehension of their ideals and methods, he would be able to judge the relative importance of each and would quickly discover that in this short life there is time for the cultivation of only the best.

The approach to such powers of discrimination obviously lies through *experience*, and to the neglect of this factor in public and private school music education, as well as to the use of insignificant musical material may be charged in great measure the present debased state of church music. No one interested in the development of music in America can fail to rejoice at the improvement which has been lately manifest in school music. Mechanical and unproductive methods are disappearing, participation by the children themselves is increasing, music is more often heard and less often talked about; and, what is quite the most important, the quality of the music sung and played is far superior to what it was twenty years ago. Much, however, still remains to be accomplished.

The argument for a sound fundamental musical education for everyone need not be put forth. In 1916 President Eliot wrote, "By many teachers and educational administrators music and drawing are still regarded as fads or trivial accomplishments not worthy to rank as substantial educational material; whereas they are important features in the outfit of every human being who means to be cultivated, efficient, and rationally happy."[1]

The decade and a half which has elapsed since these words were written has witnessed a growing conviction of their truth. With the spread of the radio and the phonograph we are realizing more and more that while there is escape from much in life that does not interest or frankly displease us, music has come to be a pretty steady concomitant of living, at the same time demanding of us the frequent exercise of a discriminating taste, if we have one. Indeed there is hardly a human activity to which music does not at some time serve

---

[1] *Changes Needed in American Secondary Education.* Publications of the *General Education Board* — Occasional Papers, No. 2.

as handmaid. It has its place in school and home, restaurant and theatre, dance-hall and public meeting place, hospital and church. Factories, even, employ it in an effort to 'speed up' production. Music is everywhere; it is inescapable. Poetry does not figure largely in our daily lives; the steady contemplation of painting and architecture is not difficult to avoid, if one so chooses; but music we have with us always. We work and play to it; it materially heightens the quality of our joys and sorrows; having lived to it we cannot consistently refuse to have it at our funerals; and it is not at all impossible that a later and enlightened medical science will decree that we shall be born to it.

The prime factor in music education, then, is taste, the fundamentals of which must be laid during the years from kindergarten through high school. In this period a child should have continuous experience of the greatest music, reinforced, at the proper time, by explanations of its style and structure and of those elements which make it really beautiful. The layman, so trained, should require no further music education in the categorical sense; the habit of associating himself with worthwhile music would take him frequently to concerts and would lead him to seek membership in amateur musical organizations. In his case we could count on the exercise of a trained musical intelligence. But how many laymen in this day can honestly lay claim to such distinction?

It may be assumed that those professional studies which under present conditions fit the musician for church work will have been undertaken fairly early in life; as a child he has doubtless shown a more than ordinary interest in music, has taken instruction in the pianoforte and later in the organ. But this, alas, far too often represents his complete stock-in-trade. His taste may be quite as bad as that of the present day musically uneducated layman; it may even be worse, in fact, if his teachers have supplied him with such material for study as is far too generally employed. He may have had no training in the structural and historical branches of music, and so he will possess neither an analytical judgment nor a reasonably comprehensive knowledge of musical literature. Frequently it happens that his first attempts at choir training are preceded by no practice or instruction in this difficult branch of his work, with the result that his initial experience is often painful and sometimes disastrous.

In the education of the church musician as in the musical training of children there has been an encouraging advance; organists and choir-masters may now procure reasonably complete instruction in all matters essential to their profession; but though the best schools of church music are contributing materially to a better standard of musicianship, it cannot be too strongly urged that instruction should unremittingly emphasize the *quality* of the music to be used and the solemn responsibility which rests upon the choir-master to select only the highest type of music for church use.

Aside from organ playing the church musician should acquaint himself with methods of choir training, correct time beating, interpretation, and the multitude of details that contribute to success in choral conducting. All this should be supported by actual practice carried on under the supervision of an experienced instructor. He should have studied theory at least through the simple orders of counterpoint; he should be acquainted with the history of music, particularly with those periods, schools, and composers most fruitful in great church music; he should have such analytical and critical knowledge as would enable him to select for his church a truly distinguished library of music; and this knowledge, together with all the rest of his equipment, should be bulwarked by a theory of the object of church music which should dominate his every professional act.

All this is a minimum requirement, but even so one may wonder how many church musicians even approach such an ideal of attainment. Are they not too often chosen by the music committee solely for their proficiency in organ playing; for a charming personality that lessens the rigors of choir practice and adds to the numbers of the chorus; for a lusty voice, which, exercised in the hymns, encourages the believer to do his vocal bit?

There is no warrant for assuming that the minister's

musical taste is better than the layman's.   The clergyman, while in college, may have taken a course in
music appreciation and history, but such slight intellectual adornment as this training may provide can
hardly be weighed against the experience gained in the
earlier musically arid years of school.   It is obvious
that the minister needs for his work no such comprehensive training in music as does his organist, but in
view of the extensive part which music plays in the
service it is difficult to understand its consistent neglect by theological schools.   Music is admittedly a
problem of the ministry, yet seminaries offer ridiculously little training even in the practical aspects of
the subject, to say nothing of the more important
details relating to style, content, taste, and to those
principles which ought to regulate all church music
procedure.   As a layman I have no right to disparage
a knowledge of Aramaic declensions as a necessary
part of a parish minister's equipment, but I wonder
whether even a brief time stolen from such a study and
devoted to music would not in the end save many a
clergyman from painful perplexity and even, perhaps,
from an occasional twinge of conscience.   Every training school for ministers should *require* a certain amount
of musical work, some critical, some practical.   The
instruction at present offered inclines too generally in
the latter direction as represented by the teaching of
singing and organ playing.   It is far more important
that a theological student should be taught church

music ideals and that he should be furnished with the power intelligently to discriminate between good and bad church music, than that he should acquire some skill in organ playing which, in spite of common opinion to the contrary, is no guarantee of musical taste. The captain of a ship who engages an engineer to operate the machinery must, to be sure, know the capacity and function of that mechanism, but he will do better to stay on the bridge than to attempt to run the engines.

Chief among the required courses in music should be one in the appreciation of church music, which should set forth in clear terms, backed by musical illustration, the standard which ought to be demanded in churches and the reasons for the adoption of that standard. To this instruction should be added: a study of the significance of music in liturgy; work in the psychology and æsthetics of church music; at least one course in the history of church music; and one in its administration, dealing with the various types of choirs, church music finances, and the thousand and one kindred problems that young ministers now solve by bitter experience. For prospective scholars and teachers of theology the foregoing may, perhaps, be considered as works of supererogation; for the parish minister, however, they represent the minimum requirement of musical knowledge.

In speaking of the type of education which seems most necessary for the three arbiters of our church music, I have made mention of the generally inade-

quate training in music given children between kindergarten and the end of high school.   If we deplore such
education as often misdirected and ineffective, what
shall we say of the treatment accorded music in the
Sunday School?

We may well be amazed that experts in religious
education have to so great a degree overlooked music
as an aid to spiritual development.   Professor Kirsopp
Lake has pointed out that there are three ways of
cleansing the spirit: one through study, one through
saintliness, and one through association with noble
music.   Obviously the first two are not immediately
for children, but the seeds of the third cannot be too
early planted.   While the energy and vision of a few
Roman Catholics are laying the foundation of a renaissance of music within their church through the instruction of children in Gregorian chant, the Protestant
church, by ignoring the potentialities of music in the
Sunday School, is indefinitely postponing any general
improvement in the music of the church itself.[1]

In a cursory review of five works on Sunday School
administration I found no chapter in any one of them
devoted to music, and in only two was music casually,
mentioned.   It is incomprehensible that beauty which
philosophers, poets, and teachers have variously used
as a synonym for truth, religion, love, and even God

---

[1] The Junior Choir, now much cultivated in our churches, may be an important addition to church music education provided the music be of uniformly high
quality.

himself, should figure so slightly in early religious education; that in the Sunday School, the very place where the foundations of a perception of the good and the beautiful theoretically are laid, pictures and music should play a negligible part. Perhaps the prime cause of the appalling state of Sunday School music is the tenacity with which we cling to the fallacy that the musical receptivity of children is limited to the trivial and the immediately attractive. It is an educational truth many times proved that children will sing, and will love to sing, and will listen attentively to good music quite as readily as to bad. If only we could once and for all persuade ourselves that children do not see through the eyes nor hear through the ears of grown-ups. A child's musical taste is a blank page whereon anything may be inscribed. His capacity for appreciation is far more sensitive and plastic than ours which is thickly set about with prejudice and association. Yet when we undertake to deal with the religious training of children through music, we begin by assuming that because they are children they must be approached as we would approach the lowest order of adult intelligence.

Those who would offer better music to the Sunday School need not be in the least concerned that the child does not intellectually grasp to the full the significance of the music he hears, nor that he is unable to take part expertly in the musical exercises of the session. To quote from Fuller-Maitland . . . "each of us can realize that in early life we were often impressed by things inherently big that we could not at once appreciate or apprehend, and these kinds of impressions, like acquired tastes, are very apt to remain with us through life, being strengthened, not weakened, as 'knowledge grows from more to more.'"[1]

Now, complete disbelief in the beneficial effect of good music upon the young is nowhere more clearly shown than in the music of the hymns selected for the Sunday School. Suppose the littlest children cannot actually sing the melody of a great and simple hymn, what of it? It is enough that they should *try* as they often will, or failing that, that they should listen to the older pupils and to the teachers thereby early acquiring an experience which will grow into active participation in the later years of Sunday School and church. Far better, I say, that not a note should be uttered by the children than that they should be fed upon those musical all-day 'suckers' which customarily grace that section of the hymnal labelled "For the Young." Such tunes are Samuel Smith's *Edengrove* ("There's a Friend for little children") and Barnby's *Children's Praise* ("Wilt thou hear the voice of praise"); but most notable among these musical and literary parodies is *St. Theresa*, sung to "Brightly gleams our banner," a Sunday School constant in a field of similarly worthless variables. Sullivan, perhaps, designed

---

[1] *The Need for Reform in Church Music.*   J. A. Fuller-Maitland.   Published in *Church Music Society* — Occasional Papers, No. 1.

that tune for *Ruddigore* or *The Pirates*, but, sensing its musical poverty, consigned it to the hymnal where it has gone on vitiating the taste of generations of children. There are numbers of good and not difficult hymns which children can and, under enlightened Sunday School administration, do sing: *L'Omnipotent; Nun Danket; Ein Feste Burg; Sine Nomine; Jesu, der du Selbsten Wohl; Hyfrydol; Creation*, and a multitude of others.

Essentially the same attitude of distrust in the range and power of the childish imagination and in youthful aptitude for laying hold of the fundamentals of beauty is displayed in the texts of Sunday School hymns. We need not, of course, choose hymns whose texts are crowded with polysyllabic words, which set forth some abstract aspect of theology, nor need we follow the precept of an earlier age which delighted in hymns of intense introspection like the following, drawn from *The Christian Lyre*, a book much recommended for religious exercise in the middle nineteenth century:

> "Ah, lovely appearance of death,
>   What sight upon earth is so fair?
>   Not all the gay pageants that breathe
>   Can with a dead body compare;
>   With solemn delight I survey
>   The corpse, when the spirit is fled;
>   In love with the beautiful clay,
>   And longing to lie in its stead."

The morbidity of such a hymn must have been repellant even to a generation inured to literary horrors. It is pretty bad poetry and it portrays a wholly unnatural state of mind. But is it, in these particulars, markedly worse than

"There's a rest for little children
Above the bright blue sky,
Who love the blessed Saviour,
And to the Father cry;
A rest from every turmoil,
From sin and sorrow free,
Where every little pilgrim
Shall rest eternally."

or

"Brightly gleams our banner,
Pointing to the sky,
Waving wanderers onward
To their home on high."

or "Beauteous are the flowers of earth," three verses of which began with the words, "Yes, he will"?

It is not necessary to furnish children with hack verses simply because they are children. Just as we know that a child may be deeply impressed by music which in the superiority of adult wisdom we decree as too mature for his years, so we have come to accept as pedagogically sound the principle that children do not need to understand the literal meaning of every word they sing or try to sing. We can all remember the sense of awe and mystery created in us by the mere sound of certain passages from the Bible which we were required to memorize, and by the texts of the

hymns we tried to sing with our parents, the full significance of which was quite beyond us. What is wrong
with "The spacious firmament on high" as a Sunday
School hymn? It contains a few fairly long words
and the specific sense of many phrases will elude the
childish mind. But there is no real necessity for destroying the mysterious and poetic quality of such
phrases as "the spangled heavens," "the blue ethereal
sky," or "the dark terrestrial ball" by the submission
of more exact astronomical data. Phrases like "Their
great original" or "an almighty hand," which stimulate the wondrous anthropomorphisms of childhood,
need not become vehicles for the exploitation of some
denominational concept of God. Childish tongues, it
is true, will trip over words like "ethereal" and "terrestrial," but a few mispronunciations will hardly tip
the scales against the opportunity afforded children of
coming into early contact with a great religious poem
and with Haydn's noble music.

Among the worst offenders against sound church
music education is the publisher of the Sunday School
Festival Pamphlet. So at Christmastide, for example,
crowds of innocent children march up on the platforms
of a thousand American churches to sing slippery tunes
which need only a few accessories to transport one to
the night clubs of Harlem. It is not conceivable that
Sunday School superintendents would permit this sacrilege if it were obvious. That they don't perceive
it is largely due to a lack of musical taste and, in some

part at least, to the ensnaring mendacity of the title
page.   What wreckage music publishers have wrought
through the beguiling nature of those Sunday School
pamphlet covers!   Look in your cabinet and I am
sure you will find at least one, bearing the representation of an anæmic child in a night-gown holding a
palm in his hand; the fraility of his physique due, perhaps, to enforced subsistence on the musical contents
of the pamphlet he adorns.   "With such an assurance
of piety vouchsafed me on the title page, why," says
the superintendent, "should I trouble to look within?"
And he doesn't; from which fact it results that the
typical Sunday School music pamphlet is probably
without a parallel in musical mediocrity.   As educational error, however, the average Sunday School hymnal runs it a close second, is, indeed, literally panting
at its heels.   Neither the Festival pamphlet nor the
Sunday School hymn-book are necessary.   A good
church hymnal will be found to contain abundant material for Sunday School use.

Individualism

If only there were some imminent likelihood that
the indifferent and complacent would awaken to the
responsibility that is theirs to improve education for
the benefit of church music, a long step forward would
have been taken.   But unfortunately quite the reverse
is the case.   Take the layman, for example, the most
powerful factor in the problem.   He is in a position
to dictate the course of church music because he is

numerically superior and he pays the bills. He says he doesn't know much about music (by which he means that he does not play the piano) but he knows what pleases him. And if you tell him that the church music he likes is not only bad music but profane as well and that he is guilty of near-sacrilege in countenancing its performance, he becomes very indignant, as any good American would, and says he doesn't consider it anybody's business what his taste is and he doesn't propose to let a high-brow tell him what he ought or ought not to prefer; the music suits him, it makes him feel good, and that's enough.

We live in an age of individualism where art occupies a place remote from the significance and dignity which was bestowed upon it by older civilizations. Since the war, striking examples of our individualistic attitude toward all branches of art appear from time to time, and in order to prevent the committing of artistic atrocities, many municipalities now require that all memorials such as fountains, monuments, tablets, and the like, shall be passed upon by a jury of art experts before the object in question shall be permanently installed. Then come loud cries from prospective donors, defiant utterances, appeals to the ideal of personal liberty, the spirit of '76, or what not. All this is quite sincere, for the average man is unable to understand why his munificence should be subject to restriction since his gift can make no *physical* difference to anyone. He may be willing to labor in

behalf of good public morals, education (in the categorical sense), hygiene, or public utilities, but he does
not perceive that his failure to appreciate the importance of a community standard of beauty constitutes
an arraignment of his own public spirit.   Popularly
speaking, music is a by-product of activity and not an
end in itself.   It will be many a day, I fear, before
Americans generally perceive that beauty is, indeed,
an integral part of the moral order; and I am sure that
it would be difficult, or even impossible, at present to
persuade the American layman that his tolerance of
unworthy music in church or elsewhere constitutes an
offence either against society or against God.

Individualism among church musicians arises generally from a narrow or limited musical training.   I
can think of but few musicians, who, having been ex-
posed to good church music over a period of years,
deliberately threw away their talents on the cheap and
the mediocre.   To pronounce them opportunists would
be uncharitable.   They are, perhaps, sufferers from
paralysis of the discriminatory function; musicians who
are congenitally incapable of perceiving what is good
and what is bad.   Yet there are others whose gifts are
not thus limited who have no desire to educate themselves or to strive for the establishment of healthier
church music conditions.   Like the layman who resents any imputation of inferiority in æsthetic out-
look, the church musician generally stiffens against
any suggestion that there is a better musical country

beyond.   He too refers to 'highbrow' and 'theoretical' opinion, and closes the argument with the flat
assertion that never having lost a church job he'll
back his opinion against anyone's.   Again, condemnation must not be universal.   In growing numbers of
American churches are musicians, well-educated and
endowed with a sense of responsibility, who are the
prophets of a better day.   As church music enlighten-
ment advances their ranks will inevitably and happily
increase.

Many clergymen tend to judge the quality of church
music by its effect upon their pulpit efficiency.   This
is natural but unfortunate since it leads to the application of principles in no way relating to the case, particularly where clerical displeasure centers on performance.   Sloppy organ playing or indifferent singing may
well affect a man's preaching, but this is, in reality, a
superficial consideration.   Surely it is not the function
of church music to supply the minister with inspiration.   The best church music is capable of doing just
that, but whether it succeeds or not depends not on its
character or performance but upon the clergyman himself.   Incidentally no greater slight may be cast upon
the dignity of church music or upon the sincerity of
the musicians than to praise in public either music
or performance.   By the same token the most eloquent
tribute to the complete effectiveness of noble church
music which I have ever witnessed befell after a none
too smooth performance of Byrd's "The souls of the

righteous," when a clergyman of rare discernment, evidently much moved and sensing the fact that after such transcendent music, however performed, any spoken word would forever destroy a moment of unearthly serenity, forebore to read the prescribed lesson and knelt in silent prayer. This man, for once at least, had borne in upon him the fundamental fact that the question of good or bad church music is settled not by *means* but by *substance*. What constitutes appropriateness of substance is too often determined, however, by the personal preference of the individual for a certain type of music quite apart from its technical make-up and the associations which surround it, or by confused thinking which embraces almost any type of music as eligible to be included within the category of 'church music.' Perhaps the most striking example of tangled opinion on this matter comes from Liszt, who, speaking for himself and Berlioz, said: "For want of a better term we may well call the new music Humanitarian. It must be devotional, strong, and drastic, uniting — on a colossal scale — the theatre and the church, dramatic and sacred, superb and simple, fiery and free, strong and calm, translucent and emotional."[1] The man who declared "Wagner is my religion" was less inclusive but equally muddled, for the associations that group themselves about Wagner's music — associations arising from the secular quality of the text and from the conditions under which the

[1] *Gazette Musicale*, 1834, quoted in *The Oxford History of Music* (Vol. VI).

music is properly heard — are definitely secular and even theatrical. No composer, moreover, has succeeded better in supporting his text with a musical fabric of the most intensely emotional and perhaps erotic kind.

When we are in a position to impose our preferences on others the situation becomes dangerous, particularly because those preferences are generally dictated by purely emotional reactions to the music. Let us, for the moment, assume our Wagnerian enthusiast to be a parson or a music committeeman; he may, of course, insist upon the performance of Wagner at Sunday services, but if he is wise with a knowledge of the infinitely variable emotional appeal of music, he will say, "I have the greatest admiration for Wagner and he supplies for me what seem to be spiritual stimuli. On the other hand his music may, and probably does have quite a different effect upon others. Therefore, while I shall permit myself the privilege of interpreting Wagner's music as sacred whenever I hear it, in view of its secular connotations I cannot conscientiously recommend it as church music." Dogmatizing about what is good or bad church music is permissible only when supported by extensive technical equipment and reasoned theory.

Again individualism becomes rampant when there is a denominational hymn-book to be compiled. More than one editor has told me of receiving letters from clergymen reading, "I *demand* that you include the

music of such and such hymns in our church hymnal."
What right has anyone, it may justly be asked, to
place upon an editor limitations which may result in
the exclusion of material more general in application
and better for congregational singing than the particular object of some minister's musical fancy?

Tolerance walks humbly before knowledge and we
must hope for broadmindedness, at least until such
time as those in whose hands the administration of
church music is vested shall have received an education adequate to fit them for their responsibilities.

Association

Association, tradition and prejudice are three closely
allied and powerful factors which exercise a great influence on the conduct of church music; they are so inter-
dependent that it is sometimes difficult to say just
what evils ought to be attributed to any one of them,
and association, in particular, is so far-reaching in its
effect that I have thought best to reserve one aspect
of its technical application for later consideration.

No more forceful example of the power of association could be offered than the sentimental hold which
is maintained upon us by the hymns we knew as children.   Most of them were fascinatingly bad as music,
yet none of us would be willing to part with them because they are often so poignantly associated with rela-
tives and companions who are gone, with half-forgotten
places of worship, or with experiences now but dimly
recalled, and all these live far more vividly in the sound

of those old hymns than in any mere unsupported recollection of the persons or places they bring to mind. There is, of course, a timidity, a natural unwillingness to submit to cold analysis a hymn long-embedded in our experience. Do we not shrink instinctively from the pitiless scholarship that explodes those happy formulæ whose adoption we were told as children would facilitate our entry into the kingdom of Heaven? If we are fearful and even sluggish where our religious beliefs are concerned, we are even more reluctant to scrutinize critically the music that accompanies our public religious expressions.

Our youth was filled with this music and we treasure its sound as we would treasure any other sentimental link with the past. It is, moreover, an undoubted spiritual resource to older people. Only a ruthless reformer would wish to take from them a legitimate fund of inspiration and comfort. Our desire to preserve this music for them and for ourselves is not selfish; it can only be thus described when we insist on perpetuating it in the experience of children. We have a right to sing for our own edification, if we wish, such hymns as "Pull for the shore," "Let the lower lights be burning," "Nearer, my God, to Thee," or "Jesus, Lover of my soul," but we err the moment we allow the music to which they are customarily sung to be used in either church or Sunday School.

I once undertook to administer the music in a supposedly ideal Sunday School maintained by the Department of Education in a large university. The school was operated on non-denominational lines; young Episcopalians sat docilely before Unitarian teachers, and boys and girls from Fundamentalist homes received their religious instruction out of Modernist mouths. During the entire career of the school but one serious protest was registered by the parents against its administration and that concerned the only element in the instruction which could not possibly be held to be controversial, namely, the music. Exception was taken because the hymns which were being taught to the children and which they were enthusiastically singing were set to tunes unfamiliar to their elders; that the music used for those hymns was far better than that which an earlier generation had sung to the same words bore no weight. The music that had been good enough for them and for their fathers before them must, perforce, be good enough for their children. With such depressing evidences of selfishness inspired by blind association, church music in every department is full.

Again association is operative in the attitude of visiting clergymen who, upon picking up a hymnal with which they are unacquainted, select for congregational use only texts and tunes which *they* know but with which the congregation very possibly may not be acquainted. These men will inquire of an organist why he played "The Church's One Foundation" to *Dank sei Gott* when it is *always* sung to *Materna*, forgetting apparently that even in any one hymnal the same words are often presented with more than one musical setting and that there is absolutely no warrant for assuming a single union of text and music. These clergymen overlook the fact that the musical traditions of the parish they are visiting may be represented by a repertory of hymn-tunes quite different from their own and far superior in musical quality. With almost childish ingenuousness they hunt for 'something everyone can sing', when, in reality, their choice may be unfamiliar, having been replaced by a better tune to the same words. When one considers that *Duke Street* occurs at least four times in any good hymn-book, and that the words of "O little town of Bethlehem" are sung to three 'familiar' tunes, it is obvious that within certain limits of musical character any poem will go to any tune of the same metre.

Association when applied to funeral hymns is a different matter. Here it is not reasonable to expect those that mourn to sacrifice the comfort which a particular tune or text can give. In the case of "For all the saints" however, usage is bringing about the frequent and salutary substitution of Vaughan Williams' noble *Sine Nomine* in place of the bromidic and lachrymose *Sarum*. For an increase in such healthy replacements and for a greater willingness to sacrifice even our dearer associations in behalf of better church music let us earnestly hope.

Tradition

If we may call association the godfather of mediocrity, we must ascribe a nearer relationship to tradition.
And first it is in the matter of hymns again that we
find tradition disagreeably active.   Heaven knows
that congregational part-singing of the best known
hymns is generally feeble.   Most people are at their
musical best when uniting with others on the melody,
whereas the churchgoer who conscientiously attempts
to read and sing the part to which his high school
teacher once assigned him (though he is probably
something else or nothing by now) usually contrib-
utes, with those in like case, nothing more than a
dejected droning.   If congregations could be induced
to sing the melodies of more chorals or even to sing
their familiar hymns in unison, some gain in the assurance and the volume of the singing would ensue.
To be sure, many a churchgoer who shouts with abandon in his bathtub is struck dumb with self-conscious-
ness at the idea of even murmuring a hymn-tune, and
if the hymn is not one of the dozen or so really thorough-
going familiar tunes, he behaves as a turtle does when
someone unexpectedly taps on its shell.   Stolid refusal even to try to sing a new hymn is, forsooth, a
tradition in many American churches.   If, to a class
of youngsters, you sang a simple melody six times and
discovered that even then those children could not
utter one note of it, you would either discipline them
for insubordination, or stand them in the corner to

wear fools' caps. Yet your adult layman, who will insist that congregational participation is the core of Protestant worship, will listen with apparent concentration to a new and simple tune, will follow with evident concern the progress of the melody from note to note through six verses, and at the end will still be inarticulate. And quite unconscious that he is a self-condemned dunce he will object that the hymn was not familiar. The lines

> "Sometimes a light surprises
> The Christian as he sings"

were probably not written in a spirit of facetiousness, but reading them, and thinking of the great silent Protestant congregation, it is difficult to keep a straight face. Even the occasional appearance of that mysterious beam would help somewhat to lighten the total vocal eclipse which has settled down on lay participation in the music of the service.

In the Episcopal church there is a tradition for assigning to the choir certain parts of the service such as the *Te Deum* and the *Magnificat*. This custom is doubly unfortunate as it leads to an exclusively choral performance of texts which are primarily congregational and it generally introduces what are to all intents and purposes concert settings. Ideally considered, there is comparatively little part-music set to the canticles and other similar divisions of the rite which is even a fair musical match for the literary quality of the texts and which is, at the same time, of suitable service length.   At present, the congregation having risen, enjoys what appears to be a long seventh inning stretch, while the choir launches out in extended vocal flights involving senseless repetitions of text, to the end that much time is wasted, some mediocre music is heard, and the Protestant principle of "let *all* the people praise Thee" is delivered another body blow.   The congregation ought either to read or sing its own parts of the service; and if the latter, plainsong should be used, as it moves with comparative rapidity, is easy to learn, employs no unnecessary repetition of text and is, withal, supremely beautiful.

In many churches there is a tradition for performing an anthem or organ solo during the collection. It would be interesting to know where and when this custom came into being.   The offertory is in the nature of a sacrament and it resents any attempt to heighten its significance by distraction of any sort. Music during a wedding service, a funeral, the taking of communion, or of the offertory is an impertinence. The solemn import of these demands entire concentration and in the noblest liturgies they receive it.   In these liturgies music is never incidental but is always a part of a continuous and integrated whole.   Our Protestant devotion to 'a little something on the organ' may be accounted for in part by our desire to inject apparent unity into a disjunct array of prayers, notices, scripture readings and so forth, and in part by the nervous impatience provoked in us by silence. In this connection I cannot do better than to quote Mr. Sydney Nicholson:[1]

"Another reason why the voluntary, or its younger brother the interlude, is employed is our supposed extraordinary dislike of silence in church. There is a tendency apparent in most churches to fill up every single corner of the Service with some sort of sound: not only must we have a voluntary while the choir come in — it must last precisely until they have risen from their knees; a few bars must be added at the end of the Psalms if the priest has not yet reached the lectern — he could not possibly walk there without an instrumental accompaniment; if the collection lasts longer than its accompanying hymn (why always sing a hymn while the faithful are fumbling for their threepenny pieces?), it would be outrageous not to go on playing until the churchwardens have returned to their seats; even the final words of peace do not seem to enjoin as much as ten seconds of silence, and if we have not to endure the sentimental trivialities of a vesper hymn, we must be thankful to escape with a few more or less innocuous chords on the *Voix Célestes*, even though the harmonies may be incorrect and the progressions inconsequent.

If only those in authority would realize the value of occasional silences in our Services, how great the gain would be!   The continual use of music to fill up all the vacant spaces in the Service gives a sense of restlessness and a lack of deliberation which is sometimes almost painful.   It produces the same sort of effect as a hurried rendering of the Service: as if the congregation could not be kept waiting for a few seconds, but everything must be timed to fit in like clockwork.   It tends to make the whole thing seem artificial, and a performance rather than an act of worship.   Needless pauses are of course not advocated, but they are almost better than needless sounds."

Even more difficult to understand is the hallowed tradition that has gathered about such phrases as

[1] Published in *Church Music Society* — Occasional Papers, No. 6.

'sacred anthem,' 'church music,' and the like.   In all
fields, the church excepted, there are definite criteria,
such as are set by style, formal considerations, degree
of difficulty, and so forth, which place a piece of music
within a certain area of designation, such as dance
music, opera, or symphony.   But with church music
the tradition is as follows: A composer selects a sacred
text to which he sets music.   It is probable that few
composers of the modern anthem write without hope
of publication or profit.   That is, perhaps, natural in
our time.   He makes his music, therefore, pleasing,
popular, if you will.   The publisher sees commercial
possibilities in the piece and brings it out; first, however, taking the precaution to label it 'Sacred Anthem.'   Its musical substance may be quite as secular as a love-song, but few will be found to question
its right to be called 'church music' as long as it bears
upon its front page the magic password 'sacred anthem.'   In this apparently prophetic ascription of the
title 'sacred music' to all music with sacred texts we
are reminded of Eve's method of naming the animals
as related in Mark Twain's *Eve's Diary*.   "Whenever a new creature comes along, I name it before he
(Adam) has time to expose himself by an awkward
silence.   In this way I have saved him many embar-
rassments.   I have no defect like his.   The minute I
set eyes on an animal I know what it is.   I don't
have to reflect a moment; the right name comes out
instantly, just as if it were an inspiration, as no doubt

it is, for I am sure it wasn't in me half a minute before. I seem to know just by the shape of the creature and the way it acts what animal it is." So church music becomes the child of the publisher's fancy, and the publisher himself the capricious primal mother of musical criticism. Not all publishers, however, are undiscriminating. Honor to those who are bringing out reprints of the church classics and the best of the modern Russian and English output. To them we owe a debt of sincerest gratitude.

As continued and bitter experience prove what an implacable foe to music architecture can be, one marvels at the paradox that these two, whose inner characteristics are so similar, should ever be at war. In music we speak of 'design,' 'structure,' 'plan,' 'detail' and 'ornamentation;' musical compositions are sometimes named for the major types of architecture, and occasionally we speak of some great building as 'frozen music.' However æsthetically questionable such an interchange of description and terminology may be, the strong ties which bind music and architecture together are undeniable. Must we conclude that there is something fundamentally antipathetic in these two arts, or is it simply where the church is concerned that they dwell in unhappy union? In view of the many splendid buildings which offer the most favorable auspices for the hearing of secular music, is it not possible that architects, and not architecture, are to blame?

It would be interesting to know how many practis-

ing architects have had any training whatsoever in
the matter of properly equipping a church for music;
in such details as the amount of space necessary for
the housing of an organ adequate to the needs of the
building; in the proper height and most effective design and location of organ chambers; in the best situation for the console; in the most desirable type of
library case for organ and choir music; in choir robing-
room facilities; in the acoustic arrangements most favorable for choir singing; and, of the first importance,
how large a choir-loft ought to be to contain a choir of
average size.   These, and many other details, are customarily left to the ignorance of the architect or to the
whim of the building committee to decide.   Often the
actual construction of churches is so far advanced
before someone with adequate knowledge is consulted
that any prospect of proper organ installation or of
decent facilities for choir performance is out of the
question.   The old-fashioned method of attaching the
console to the body of the organ with the choir standing behind the organist is obviously ridiculous; yet
architects still plan organs and choir galleries in that
way.   Similarly impractical are those copies of English chapels where the organist dwells in the second
story completely insulated from contact with his choir
below.   All sorts of evasions are practiced to escape
the patent folly of such an arrangement, but they are
evasions, and they usually result in the mute acceptance of the accompanied anthem as inevitable, or in

the organist's sounding a chord and then legging it down the stairs to conduct his choir.

Now all these makeshifts arise primarily from the perfectly natural emphasis which the architect places on the eye; but it is certain that for practical, if for no other reasons, the ear must, in church architecture, receive some consideration.   It is apparently an axiom that a church favorably constructed for speaking is unfriendly to music; that is, if a building is sufficiently resonant to supply the illusive effect which is inherent in the best church music, preaching will be difficult to understand; and as, in our Protestant service, preaching is paramount, many buildings are deadened by the use of acoustic plaster and heavy carpets to a point where good singing is quite ineffective and singing on pitch all but impossible.

Never, I believe, was music more brutally slaughtered to make an architectural Roman holiday than in the case of a large metropolitan church whose interior is, indeed, a noble work, but whose musical arrangements suggest that the architect had been hopelessly embittered by a tragic love affair with some lady organist and was here having one vast diabolical fling at the entire guild.   The player sits at his console in a room built off the chancel.   He receives the sound of the music in two distinct waves: first, the singing of the choir, and second, the sound of the organ, part of which is above his head, but separated from him by a ceiling, the other part being situated across the aisle from the organist's 'sitting room.' It is plain that the player must strike the organ well in advance of the reception of either sound wave. Competent observers of the efforts of an untried organist to accompany an anthem under these circumstances report the result as bearing a close resemblance to a well-developed case of St. Vitus' dance. Architectural monstrosities like the church I have described are fortunately rare, but far too many modifications of them do exist.

Of the persistent obsessions tending to hamper musical efficiency, none is more general than the chancel so arranged that half the choir sits on one side and half on the other. The great majority of Episcopal churches in this country are so constructed, yet I have never found a choir-master who, dissociating himself from the kind of thinking that invariably sees church music as isolated from all other music, believed that such an arrangement was ideal for musical performance. Whatever its architectural reason, there are two obvious objections to such a scheme. First, no body of singers is ideally situated when it is split in two sections. Such an arrangement generally forces the sopranos and tenors to face the altos and basses across the chancel, whereas it is invariably easier for neighboring parts, such as soprano and alto, tenor and bass, to be compactly located; they are naturally related, and in the case of a divided chancel it often happens that they cannot hear each other consistently. Second, the choir-master, even if he leaves his bench in order to direct, is visible to only one-half of his choir. To escape this dilemma it is customary to employ a deputy facing the choir-master, whose function it is to relay the conductor's motions; or to rig up a system of mirrors which make the chancel reminiscent of some corner of an amusement park, or of a woman's boudoir. At any distance neither a deputy nor mirrors can reflect the choir-master's all-important facial expressions or his silent transmissions of the text. Another solution of the problem takes the conductor into the middle of the chancel where he is visible to all his choir, but that particular '*deus ex machina*' is, perhaps, the least desirable of all because the spectacle of a conductor inevitably suggests a secular concert. To avoid all these difficulties the harried choir-master, when his choir is not too large to allow it, wisely cuts the Gordian knot by concentrating all the singers on one side of the chancel, thus gaining unity and complete intelligible visibility.

Now music *will* work in divided chancels, and there are many good choirs which occupy them on Sunday. This does not in the least, however, alter the fact that the situation is difficult and unnatural from a musical point of view. The tradition descends from the period when the clergy, and not the modern choir, occupied the chancel, and when singing by the clergy was no such complicated or imposing matter as is the choir singing of to-day. Why, then, do churches still insist upon inflicting on choirs and choir-masters this illogical arrangement? Merely because architects have decreed that it conforms to their canons of beauty, because it is almost an architectural truism where a certain type of church is concerned, and because choirs *can*, if they have to, sing under such conditions. The divided chancel is a positive example of what I mean when I say that church music is not looked upon as *music*, but as a special branch of musical activity, governed by all imaginable considerations except purely musical ones. For no architect nor musician undertaking the design of a building in which music was to play an important part would for a moment think of creating an arbitrary situation in which a chorus was forever forced to sing in two separate sections; and no chorus, the church choir excepted, ever does so sing. For antiphonal singing, choruses are occasionally placed on opposite sides of a platform or at the front and back of a building. The ordinary chancel is not wide enough to permit effective responsive singing, but just wide enough to prevent the choirs from singing as a unit.

There is a good deal to be said for locating the organ and choir at the rear of the church; the main objection to this, however, is that it emphasizes a tendency now far too prevalent, namely, that of segregating the musical ministry from the clerical ministry, with the result that the musicians come to be considered, and to consider themselves, as an extra-ministerial professional or amateur group whose duty it is to supply musical interludes to the service. The ideal situation for the organ and choir is behind the chancel, veiled by some sort of screening device from the view of the congregation. Music is for the ear and for the ear alone, and any involving of the eye results in false values and a loss of music's true function, and nowhere is this principle more profoundly true than in the church.

Placed as I have just described, the choir may be grouped as a unit and may give itself over wholeheartedly to its office without consciousness of being on review. The choir-master, too, is free to conduct his choir naturally, not scrunched down behind a choir stall, nor forced to relay his motions at long distance or with the aid of refractive devices.

Architectural obsessions, such as the divided chancel and other unnatural musical layouts, directly affect the selection of service music in two ways: by placing upon the musical ministry the burden of working under needlessly difficult conditions, and by perpetuating the tyranny of the accompanied anthem. Let us tactfully ignore the fact that the accompanied anthem is the sure retreat of the lazy choir-master and of the choir that would avoid rehearsal; none the less, cautious and conscientious choir-masters are not entirely to be blamed for looking upon it as insurance against vocal disasters resulting not from conditions of their own making, but originating in the ignorance and traditional attitude of some architect. While a

mixture of accompanied and unaccompanied anthems
is desirable, we would all agree, I trust, that unaccompanied church singing is more effective than accompanied, and that a large majority of the best church
music was designed for *a cappella* performance.   Guilds
of organists and associations of church musicians everywhere might immeasurably benefit a bad situation by
undertaking a campaign to induce schools of architecture to introduce into their curriculums instruction in
matters which affect church music in all its branches.

Prejudice

Of the many unfortunate personal attitudes which
hamper church music, none is more stubborn than
prejudice.   Take, for example, the Protestant opposi-
tion to Plain-song.   This attitude is founded partly
in the fact that Plain-song is simple unison chant,
unmetrical, at its best when unaccompanied, and distinctly archaic in character due to its modal make-up.
It is not concert music and it is not beguiling to the ear;
but every musician recognizes it as the most poignant
expression of the religious ideal in all music.   Its general rejection by Protestants is mainly due not to its
unfamiliarity nor its lack of sensuous appeal, but to its
primary possession by the Roman Church.   It seems
to us to breathe the very Catholic doctrine, and though
everyone will agree that music, apart from words, cannot teach, and though the dignity and extra-worldli-
ness of Plain-song is above that of any type of music
now heard in our Protestant churches, yet it belongs

to the Catholics and, therefore, we will have none of it. The same logic would quite as justly lead us to abstain from eating fish, especially on Fridays.

But better arguments than prejudice, which is, in reality, no argument at all, may be advanced against the use of Latin; for it is a Protestant tradition and a wholesome one, that services shall be spoken and sung in the vernacular. On the other hand, many Latin texts, even taken literally, are not ungrateful to Protestant dogma. Any language loses by translation, and where no satisfactory translation exists, or where a good paraphrase or substitute text is not to be had, there is no reason why choirs in Protestant churches should not sing in Latin. In the Middle Ages and in the sixteenth century, music and text were one and indivisible; every shade and accent of the Latin found their complement in the musical setting, and to separate these does violence to both music and words. All this is offered merely for what it is worth, but in view of the lengths to which translators and adaptors go in their zeal merely to be rid of Latin as Latin, the foregoing facts ought to be taken into consideration.

A prejudice so childish that one hesitates to speak of it is that which decrees that the organist and choirmaster of an Episcopal church shall be an Episcopalian. It is possible to sympathize with a desire that he be moral and a Christian, but why must the first consideration be his allegiance to the Episcopal church? Is it not of greater importance that he be a good musician with a thorough respect for the finest ideals of Christian music?   If he has had time to acquire this and at the same time achieve the estate of Episcopalianism, well and good.   He isn't a better musician because he is an Episcopalian, and competence ought to come before confirmation.   Far easier to understand is the prejudice against admitting non-Christians to musical office; for church musicians are co-ministers in the carrying on of the service, and at first thought it seems incongruous to invite as participants organists or singers who are not of the Christian faith. None the less it is surprising that those who see Christianity as the only road to salvation, fail to observe in the presence of non-Christians in a Christian choir an unexampled opportunity to preach the true doctrine to those without the fold.   Are these good Christians not a little remiss, perhaps, in their missionary obligations?

But the most widespread and, to music by far the most harmful prejudice, is that which to a great extent excludes from Protestant public worship those factors which tend to stimulate the imagination.   Throughout the life of the Roman church her poetry, music, architecture and ritual have concerned themselves primarily with the imagination of the worshipper, leaving the rational and the didactic to the sphere of teaching and preaching.   That church holds, and rightly, I believe, that a sense of the presence of God is most quickly stimulated by significant beauty and appropriate action, and that it is a small step from awareness of the Divine Presence to contemplation of the Divine Mystery. In the Catholic service preaching is by no means paramount. Sharply contrasted with the Roman ideal of worship is that of the typical nonconformist congregation which relegates all means of grace to a position of relative unimportance compared with the sermon. That Protestantism is not unanimous in its approval of this state of affairs is evidenced in the recent appointment of a Committee on Worship by The Federal Council of the Churches of Christ in America. The aims of the Committee as defined by the Council's Administrative Committee are as follows:

(a) To provide a central clearing-house for the various denominations for consultation, for interchange of experience, plans and methods, for mutual reinforcement and stimulus, and for joint study as to what is needed to cultivate the spirit and practice of worship in the Protestant churches.

(b) To provide a leadership in the field of worship for those denominations which do not have any special committees of their own dealing with this subject, but which feel the need for assistance.

(c) To provide a center for publishing articles or other materials that it is believed will be equally useful in many denominations.

(d) To use the religious press as a channel for calling attention to the more important materials produced by the various denominational agencies or by others engaged in the study of worship.

Some idea of the convictions which suggested the Committee's appointment may, perhaps, be offered by quotations from an article[1] on this subject written by Bishop Wilbur Thirkield, of the Methodist Episcopal Church and Chairman of the Council's Committee on Worship:

"There is evident a new liturgical life awakening throughout all Christendom giving a fresh and vital interest in worship.   The quest is for a return to the liturgical ideas of the Early Church, reviving the spirit of true worship. . . . Let us face two facts: first, that in the churches where the pulpit has held the center and worship has been subordinated, *church attendance has declined.* . . . The second fact to face is, that in representative cities, east and west, Methodist Episcopal and Baptist churches have been surpassed in growth by denominations in which worship is emphasized and marked by reverence and devoutness."

In the same article the writer cites the opinion of his fellow-Bishop Francis McConnell as stated in his Yale lectures on *The Prophetic Ministry*. "Ritualistic worship, properly conceived, aims at institutionally gathering up for daily use the insights and emotions which arise from the prophets' moral activities." Of like tenor is the statement of Professor James Bissett Pratt:[2]

"The worshipper in the Protestant church must be made to feel, as the Catholic feels at the Mass, that *something is really being done* — something in addition to the change in his own consciousness.   Let him understand that you wish him to come to church in order that you may make a psychological impression on him, and he will be increasingly likely to stay away.   Or he may come to hear your opera singer, but his religious sentiment will remain untouched.   If public worship is to be profitable to him, he must find in it something more than that."

---

[1] *Spiritual Power Through Worship in the Sanctuary.*   Published in *The Christian Advocate*, February 19, 1932.

[2] *The Religious Consciousness.*   James Bissett Pratt.

And again:

"There is a kind of worship that is perfectly objective and sincere and that is quite as possible for the intelligent man of to-day as it was for the ancient — namely, that union of awe and gratitude which is reverence, combined perhaps with consecration and a suggestion of communion, which most thoughtful men must feel in the presence of the cosmic forces and in reflecting upon them."[1]

At present, Protestant services may be divided into two classes: first, those of the Episcopal church, especially the high church, which make beauty and the suggestive power of symbolism integral elements of worship; and second, those of the non-conformist congregations, which center about preaching, and which depend not at all for their sanction upon what their sponsors term the 'externals' of religion. Many reasons may be assigned for the denial of a place for beauty in Protestant worship, such as the instinctive reaction against a vital factor in Roman Catholic religious observance, the desire to create a democratic type of service which shall emphasize spiritual equality, which shall be grateful to the 'average' man, and which recognizes the antipathy generally expressed by such a man toward anything, whether in his house or in his church, which savors of 'putting on the dog;' and the tendency to rationalize everything in religion to a point where any factor involving the use of the imagination would be not only out of place, but would be, as well, a distraction from the business in hand.

[1] *The Religious Consciousness.* James Bissett Pratt.

In a plea for the retention of significant adjuncts to the service of the Church of England, an anonymous writer says:[1]

"If the marvels of architecture and sculpture, of glass and woodwork, of music and liturgy, which have long adorned our churches, are but luxurious corruptions of the spirit, by all means let them perish. If, on the other hand, they are the very symbol and expression of that Christian life which has nothing in common with a business career, let us boldly assert that to sacrifice them to any popular outcry, with or without the Church, would be not merely a blunder, but a crime."

Acquaintance with the quiet dignity of the services of the Church of England ought to inform any religiously sensitive person that the significant adjuncts to worship which the writer mentions are anything but "luxurious corruptions of the spirit."

Of the two orders of service to which I referred a moment ago, one is religious, that is, it revolves about God as the animating center; the other is ethical, and concerns itself with man. They range from the highest Anglo-Catholic mass to the church in Weatherford, Texas, where the preacher wears overalls in the pulpit "in order that the workingman with limited means may feel at home in his church."[2] It is not the function of this book to argue in behalf of either type, but to say under what service conditions music operates most successfully, and under what conditions it is a stranger in a strange land.

[1] *The Choral Foundations in the Church of England.* Published in *Church Music Society* — Occasional Papers, No. 8.

[2] *Boston Traveler*, April 14, 1932.

Now, from the lay point of view, the most satisfactory definitions of religion are those which emphasize the elements which no wisdom can explain: the mystery of the Godhead, the divine ordering of the universe, human salvation, life after death, and those other eternal queries before which reason and experience are helpless. And it is exactly here, where the logic of human speech is futile that the language of music is most eloquent. What faith is to religion, imagination is to music; and as no faith is worthy of the name which has not some intellectual background, so the vague pleasures of music unsupported by some knowledge of music itself constitute the lowest form of musical enjoyment. As the best part of religion can neither teach nor explain, so music also is helpless in these particulars; as religious exercise is at its best when it glorifies the intangible, so the music of the church reaches its greatest heights when it seeks to fulfill no practical purpose. Indeed, the more worship points man away from earth and toward God, the greater is its power; and in the same way the more music shuns the everyday idiom of man's musical experience, the more efficient partner of worship it becomes. For music, like religion, is fundamentally a mystery. Indeed, you can no more account for what makes music beautiful or what is the nature of the inspiration that prompted that music, than you can explain the divine mercy.

If, then, you are determined to do nothing in your service which the Catholics do, or if you are going to preserve in your worship the sense of man's six-day life in the world, or if you wish to celebrate on Sunday a practical and ethically profitable plan of life; in other words, if you do not believe that worship in great measure gains in value exactly in proportion to its remoteness from the secular, you may as well use secular music in your churches, which is, in effect, what a great many Protestant churches do.   But by pursuing any of the foregoing ideals, you take from music those imaginative and suggestive qualities which make it a particularly valuable ally to religious exercise.

I am inclined to think that behind the particular wish to democratize worship lies the typical self-conscious American attitude toward beauty in general.   This is by no means new, nor has it always been exclusively characteristic of our own church.   The sterility of much late sixteenth and seventeenth century German Protestant music has been ascribed to this very distrust of the spiritual efficacy of beauty; and we may reasonably inquire whether the artistic pessimism of seventeenth century England has not been reborn in this country.   Among a great many Americans a serious regard for beauty is taken as a sign of weakness. Those who frequent art galleries and concerts of classical music are regarded as 'high brows,' as poseurs, or as anything else that our superior Americanism employs to characterize anyone different from ourselves. At base this antagonism, implied or open, is against something undemocratic.   To have a sincere appreciation of art implies the possession of qualities of perception which constitute a kind of aristocracy of sensitiveness, against which we naturally react; indeed, the 'average' American would as readily admit being deeply moved by beauty as he would wear a monocle and don a silk hat.

Now, this 'kalophobia,' if we may invent a term, works untold harm to church music because its inevitable result is the use of music which is immediately intelligible to everyone. To use anything else implies an affectation which is undemocratic. To such an extent, indeed, have we democratized our services, that although we admit the almightiness of God, we behave in His house as though He were a friendly sort of host who, although He is God, would prefer to be treated like one of us. So we build our churches like halls; our pulpits like office desks; we must hear modernized versions of the Scriptures which sound vulgar, but which are only stupid;[1] we won't kneel when the minister prays because God, being a democratic God, respects our independence and doesn't ask such servility; we won't intone a service because a man doesn't sing to his father, he talks to him. Whatever may be the merit of such an attitude, it may be stated in behalf of a high standard of church music that no great art

[1] An eloquent example of the method by which these renderings of the Bible deliberately destroy one's sense of the difference between God and man is the substitution of "revere" for "hallowed" in the Lord's Prayer. (*The New Testament: A New Translation* by James Moffatt.) We *revere* the names of numbers of human beings, living and dead, but there is only One whose name is "hallowed."

has ever issued from any concept of God as the Supreme Benign Rotarian.

Although this book aims to set forth unwaveringly an ideal of church music which makes nothing of personal preference, I cannot refrain from pointing out that in spite of our devotion to a democratic ideal, where art, at least, is concerned, we live in an out and out aristocracy of mediocrity. Is it not the object of democracy to treat all with impartial consideration? What, then, of the lovers of good music? If they depended on the radio for the satisfaction of their tastes they would rapidly expire of artistic inanition; and that the church deliberately disregards those worshippers who are weekly thrown into a blasphemous state of mind by the musical inanities of the average service is a truism. The few distracted churchgoers usually offer no protest, but one eloquent cry of exasperation is worth recording:[1]

"If they say that the hymns (words and music) which keep me away from church draw others thither, and excite useful religious emotions, then they must take the responsibility wholly on themselves. . . . All I can urge is that they should have at least one service a week where people like myself can attend without being offended or moved to laughter."

To those, then, who deprive music of its highest qualities by ignoring the importance of beauty and imagination in the church, by omitting from worship all that they cannot explain, or by conducting their

---

[1] Published in *Church Music Society* — Occasional Papers, No. 3.

services at the level of every day life, symbolism is, of course, anathema, but anathema of a very inconsistent kind. For while in anthem and hymn we employ certain texts and phrases which are obviously cast in symbolic language, we reject without reason other specimens of literary symbolism quite as poetic and suggestive; furthermore, any effort visually to present these symbols within the church is instantly cried down. The following passages are common to Christian worship:

> "In the Cross of Christ I glory
> Tow'ring o'er the wrecks of time."

> * * * * *

> "Now from the altar of my heart
> Let incense flames arise;
> Assist me, Lord, to offer up
> Mine evening sacrifice."

> * * * * *
> "The valleys stand so rich with corn they laugh and sing."

> * * * * *
> "Here I'll raise my Ebenezer."

Ignoring the fact that the singing of a hymn containing the words "altar," "incense flames" and "evening sacrifice" represents pretty high-stepping for our Baptist and Methodist brothers, and that even the earnest Christian probably doesn't expect to be called on to go out on the nearest street corner and raise an Ebenezer (whatever that may be), the question naturally arises why some examples of symbolism are acceptable, while others are not, and why the *physical representation* of things we sing about should be hateful. The cross, for instance, is not a sign of sacrifice, it is a war-horse of the Papacy or a bit of ecclesiastical furniture; you may refer to it and sing about it, but its actual presence is offensive. Candles and vestments, both mute but eloquent reminders of common Christian principles, are viewed as senseless ornaments. The Virgin Mary is not a symbol of universal Motherhood; she is a theological error, and hymns and anthems which mention her are forbidden, with the result that quantities of the noblest sacred music are unheard in our churches. The office of the communion is in general use largely because most of us value it not as a symbol, but as a social act. It unites us as a *church* and it defines our particular *denomination*.

In view of the present state of theology and of preaching, this prejudice against symbolism is creating a hiatus between music and the remainder of the service which is far from diminishing. I speak on this matter with moderate certainty, for during the last twenty-five years, summers excepted, I have listened to an average of five sermons each week, and for a period of several years I consumed, between Sundays, not less than twelve. These were delivered by preachers representing every communion within the Protestant church. Under such conditions only the most inattentive listener could fail to observe the growing discrepancy between the theology contained in the sermon and that belonging to the anthems and hymns. To-day it is fair to say that the two often stand so far apart in a single service as to make the situation little short of ludicrous. The truth is that the greatest composers of church music have been at their best when dealing with texts which represent a type of theology not now acceptable to many Protestants. I refer not to such texts as are specifically Roman Catholic in doctrine, but to those whose import was acceptable to the evangelical branches of the Protestant church not so many years ago. Such texts, for example, as directly or indirectly deal with the salvation of the world through the death on the cross of our Lord Jesus Christ; and it is no exaggeration to say that probably not less than eighty per cent of the greatest church music centers about this theme upon which, incidentally, I have not heard a sermon preached in years.

Now, obviously, no sensible man will plead for the retention of an outworn theology merely because great poetry and great music have associated themselves with it. On the other hand, the conscientious church musician is left in a dilemma which is far from being merely theoretical; for, all questions of dogma aside, any general review of the last quarter century's preaching cannot fail to reveal that in spite of some preaching of sustained power, much sermonizing has increasingly lost that quality which is one of the richest endowments of great church music, namely, *affirmation*. If, then, evasion, uncertainty and vagueness are largely present in our preaching, with what music may we match them in the interest of a coherent service? Surely there is nothing in the musical classics of the church suitable to accompany preaching which views God as existent only in human nature and Christ as a legendary figure who left us some noble and profitable precepts of life. How many hours have I heard filled with pointless, idealistic admonitions to the richer life, to the fuller Christian character, to making the crooked straight, with never a *specific* statement as to what the richer life or the fuller Christian character are, nor just what it is that is crooked, nor exactly how to make anything straight. To these may be added discourses which are little more than lectures on the psychology of remembering and forgetting, the importance of Bible study in schools, The League of Nations, and the survival of Protestantism, down to the succession of clerical 'wise-cracks' that gain their author a humorist's reward, if nothing more.

The selection of hymns and anthems fitted to illuminate the ideas expressed in preaching is limited only by the nature of the text to which the music is set. The ideas expressed in music alone are whatever you conceive them to be. So there are innocuous and undogmatic texts which would suitably accompany any of the sermon subjects listed above; "Teach me, O Lord," "O taste and see," "And all the people saw the thunderings and the lightnings," "Except the Lord build the house," "God came from Teman," or "Behold, two blind men sitting;" but composers, unfortunately, have not been deeply stirred by texts of this kind, and for the church musician who is satisfied only with truly inspired music, they seem a pale offering indeed.

Now there are several possible solutions to this difficulty:

(1) Anthems and hymns based upon unacceptable theology may be omitted entirely from the service, as being anachronistic and having no claim to inclusion. This would result in the arbitrary elimination of much of the finest church music.

(2) Music may be confined to good congregational hymns fitted to texts whose theology is appropriate to the rest of the service.

(3) The best anthem music may be retained and suitable words substituted for those offensive to modern theology. This experiment has been tried with some degree of success. The truth is, of course, that while the sense of the completeness of the partnership between text and music is much a matter of association, it is, at the same time, impossible, where a particular text has definitely moved composers to an eloquence which fits tightly with every word, to replace that text with any other, no matter how fine, without doing violence to the integrity of the whole work.

(4) Texts and music of modified secularity may be

used to complement sermons on the movies, current plays or the modern novel.

(5) All of church music with its texts, regardless of idea or association, may be viewed as symbols of the great truths of religion and of life.

The most striking tribute to the power of symbolism I have ever known, was offered to me by one of America's foremost Unitarian clergymen, profoundly stirred by the suggestive power of Gretchaninov's setting of the Nicean Creed. "Never," said he, "would I dare allow that work to be sung in my parish church, for at the moment I, myself, am near to saying, 'Almost thou persuadest me.'" He must afterward have realized that anyone who could be led by music to change the fundamentals of his faith, never really had a faith. What he meant, obviously, was that belief, expressed with the highest affirmation, apart from any special dogmatic or even religious interpretation, can be made so eloquent through the union of resounding text and inspired music that everyone must perforce cry with them "I believe." I know full well that it is impossible for many of us to accept the statements of the Nicean Creed, but when united to noble music I can rejoice in it as I would in any mighty witness of a faith that was sure, and I can accept it as a symbol of all belief, my own included. One thing, at least, is certain; the refusal of the Protestant church to accept as symbols the great literature and beautiful music derived from alien doctrinal sources has cost her dearly;

there is, after all, a great difference between worshipping the Lord in holiness and worshipping Him in the *beauty* of holiness. And if music is to regain its former position of dignity and of comradeship with the other elements of the service, this problem of the growing disparity between the modern service of worship and the loftiest forms of church music must be squarely faced.

Disorganization

Of the attitudes and conditions with which I have been dealing, there remains only the disorganization of Protestant church music to be dealt with. Except in the case of some Episcopalian parishes where responsibility for the conduct of the music is laid upon the rector, Protestant church music is, for the greater part, carried on without benefit of direction. Theoretically, supervision is vested in music committees whose incompetence is axiomatic. Actually, the clergyman, the music committee, and the choir-master each have something to say, with the result that the Protestant church possessing an intelligent musical policy based upon reasoned theory is about as rare as a white blackbird.

An example of the divided authority which maintains is offered by those churches which employ one person to play the organ and another to conduct the choir. Absolute unity of aim and opinion in such a case is well-nigh impossible. Even with the best intentions no organist can exactly interpret the wishes of his leader; and if, as often happens, one or the other is deficient in taste, or the two are not on the best of personal or professional terms, their coöperation is not likely to be ideally productive. The double office of organist and choir-master is best administered when the responsibility belongs to a single person.

This is but a detail, however, and as an indication of the lack of coördination which exists in church music it is insignificant compared with the chaos which results from the recrimination indulged in by all the parties tangent to our problem. Consider the case of a well-known western clergyman who proclaims the present state of church music intolerable and declares that musicians are, of all men, least fitted to lead us out of Egypt. This is, of course, arrant pettishness: the Monday morning irritation of a parson whose organist during a particularly eloquent prayer accidentally stepped on the pedals with the trombone stop drawn. The offended gentleman doubtless seeks the services of a landscape architect when suffering from the toothache. Most ministers, it is fair to say, are more modest in their proclamations, but occasionally one will unburden himself to the extent of wishing that his organist would use just a little common sense! It isn't a question of taste — the man hasn't education enough of any sort to have taste — but anyone who would play the *Venusberg* music from *Tannhäuser* hasn't even common instinct. He avoids consultation and he invariably resents suggestion and criticism. He plays long after the time for the opening of the service, and his postlude is always some noisy thing regardless of the occasion. The minister would like to improve the music, but he really doesn't know enough about music to make the attempt, and, furthermore, the music committee actually controls the situation. The congregation is more interested in the so-called private lives of the choir than in the quality of the music, so the situation is pretty hopeless. But he consoles himself that most of his brother ministers are in like case.

The layman is not so reticent as the clergyman; and why, indeed, should he be? Does he not pay the choir's salaries? He is the music committee, too, and dictates the hiring and firing of the musicians. Now, in all my experience I have never known but one music committeeman whose administration was unimpeachable, and he was stone deaf. The music committee really represents the opinion of the congregation, and it exists in order to insure the congregation's getting what it wants. A music committee, if there must be one, should be composed of people who know something about music. Is membership on the finance committee eagerly bestowed upon inmates of the poor house? A man may be a first-rate banker, or an expert in pig-iron, but there is no warrant in that fact for the assumption of musical taste. If there is to be a music committee, then why not a preaching committee to regulate the tone of the minister's voice, or to limit the number of his adjectives? Simply because in the eyes of the congregation preaching, prayer, and music are

not to be dealt with on the same critical plane.   The
layman recognizes no '*lex orandi, lex cantandi,*' for there
is an unspoken authority belonging to the minister in
his field that is entirely lacking to the church musician
in his.   The layman expects the minister to teach him,
but he considers it the function of the choir-master to
give him what he wants.   He says that the choir is
paid too much and sings too little; or, if the music dis-
pleases him, he concludes that the entire organization
ought to be dismissed; and this he forthwith sets about
accomplishing.   He feels, in view of the high salaries
paid to the quartet, that the soprano ought to have
been able to produce more power on that high note
in the morning's anthem, and that the bass ought to
be made to understand that the creation of an artificial
double-chin supported by a blood-thirsty expression
such as Captain Kidd might have worn does not really
take the place of the low note he tried to make every-
body *think* he was singing.   The organist's one idea in
the hymns is to get through them as quickly as possible, and about as soon as the congregation gets geared
up to his speed, the organist branches off into an interlude after the third verse and the congregation has to
stand first on one foot and then on the other while he
indulges himself in his little game of musical solitaire.
The clergyman, thinks the layman, tends to pick out
unfamiliar and high-falutin' hymn-tunes that nobody
knows, and only last Sunday he preached so long that
they didn't get to the last hymn, which happened to

be a particular favorite of the layman's and one which his grandfather used to sing with thunderous effect. Well, he is a candidate for the music committee next year and then, you may be sure, he'll straighten these things out!

The organist always supposed that hymns were intended for the congregation to sing, but the fact is that if the quartet didn't sing them, no one would; and when they get a familiar hymn it takes half the morning to get through it because the old folks like to hang over it so; the most powerful explosive devices wouldn't propel them through "I need Thee every hour" in less than ten minutes. The organist would like to resign, but he needs the money, and the amount he receives from his church work relieves him of the necessity of giving piano lessons to Tommy Jones with an attendant saving in nervous wear and tear consequent on getting Tommy to count 1 - 2 - 3 - 4 several times in succession without causing such perturbations of the boy's mental area as would lead him to forget for a moment the averages of the four leading batsmen of the American League. The congregation, so the organist tells us, is a perfect nuisance. It comes up after every service to tell him how and what they wish he had played, and to offer advice about the quartet, the anthem, the hymns and anything else they don't happen to like. But he simply refers them to the music committee which probably knew what it wanted when it hired the quartet. None of the singers can read notes even reasonably well and only two can really sing; though if the committee was looking for lung power, as the organist suspects, it certainly got it. But the minister is the organist's greatest cross. The minister knows nothing of music and admits it, but he interferes in the administration of the music just the same. Nothing is exactly right, and he gets all his musical notions from his daughter who is supposed to be an expert because when she was in college she played in the mandolin club. The sort of music the minister raves over is usually rankly secular or the most puerile musical bosh. What would the minister think if the organist began to play before the end of the sermon or prayer the way the minister begins to talk before the organist is through playing? And he won't use any definite form to end his prayers with, so that when there comes a pause the organist thinks the minister has finished and starts the response only to discover that the pause was for breath and a few more ideas, with the result that the quartet has to subside like a punctured balloon. Oh, well, the organist proposes to hold on to this job until he can get another one, anyway.

So grinds the mill of petty criticism, and the sound of the grinding is not low. Nor was it in the past. Charges of impiety and secularity ring no more loudly in the Protestant lay conventions of London, Pittsburg, or New York, than they rang in the ecclesiastical councils of an earlier day. Individual voices were lifted then, as now, in bitter denunciation of practices that were certainly no worse than many of those now current.

"Does such oxen bellowing belong in the Church? Is it believed that God can be graciously inclined by such an uproar?"[1]

* * * * *

"Music defiles the service of religion. For the admiring simple souls of the congregation are of necessity depraved — in the very presence of the Lord, in the sacred recesses themselves of the sanctuary — by the riot of the wantoning voice, by its eager ostentation, and by its womanish affectation, in the mincing of notes and sentences."[2]

* * * * *

"Let me speake now of those who, under the show of religion, doe obpalliate the business of pleasure. . . . Whence hath the church so many organs and Musicall Instruments? To what purpose, I pray you, is that terrible blowing of Belloes, expressing rather the crakes of Thunder, than the sweetness of a voyce? Sometimes thou mayst see a man with an open mouth, not to sing, but, as it were, to breathe out his last gaspe by shutting in his breath, and by a certain ridiculous interception of his voyce to threaten silence, and now and again to imitate the agonies of a dying man, or the ecstasies of such as suffer. . . . In the meantime, the common people standing by, trembling and astonished, admire the sound of the organs, the noyse of the Cimballs and Musicall Instruments, the harmony of the Pipes and Cornets."[3]

* * * * *

"Of short time there were mere vain japes invented; descant, simple and florid counterpoint, that stirreth vain men to dancing more than to mourning. For when there are forty or fifty in a choir, three or four proud and wanton rascals will so trick the most devout service that no man shall hear the sentence and all the others will be dumb and look like fools."[4] * * * * *

[1] *Music in the History of the Western Church.* Dickinson.
[2] *Oxford History of Music* (Vol. I).
[3] *History of English Music.* Davey.
[4] Quoted in *Music and Christian Worship.* H. Walford Davies. Published in *Church Music Society* — Occasional Papers, No. 4.

"Modern church music is so constructed that the congregation cannot hear one distinct word. The choristers themselves do not understand what they are singing, yet according to priests and monks it constitutes the whole of religion. Why will they not listen to St. Paul? Music, nothing but music. There was no music in St. Paul's time. Words were then pronounced plainly. Words nowadays mean nothing. They are mere sounds striking upon the ear, and men are to leave their work and go to church to listen to worse noises than were ever heard in Greek or Roman theatre. Money must be raised to buy organs and train boys to squeal, and to learn no other thing that is good for them."[1]

*   *   *   *   *

"Our antient church music is lost, and that solid grave harmony fit for a martyr to delight in, and an Angel to hear, is now changed into a Diversion for Atheists and libertines, and that which good men can not but lament. Everything which is serious, is called in Derision, The Old Cow Path, and reputed as dull and heavy."[2]

And in our time, as well, clergyman, layman, and musician are lost in a maze of cross purposes and misunderstandings underlaid with indifference, complacency, unprotested isolation, unyielding tradition, ignorance of music, the power of individualism, the force of association, and with determined and obstructive prejudice until unity of purpose and administration is impossible. Nor is there any prospect of betterment until we deal wisely with the education of those who come after us.

[1] *Life and Letters of Erasmus.*   Froude.
[2] *The Great Abuse of Music.* Rev. Arthur Bedford, 1711, quoted in "Anthems." Cyril Bradley Rootham.   Published in *Church Music Society* — Occasional Papers, No. 7.

Part II

The Uses of Music in Worship

Music is the youngest and the least representative of
the arts.   No other force in human experience appeals
in such divers and subtle ways.   No imaginative or
emotional flight is foreign to its eloquence.   Its versatility and pervasiveness are so much a matter of
common knowledge that we accept music as an un-
questioned member of the immediate family of our
experiences; and much as familiarity often breeds a
species of carelessness that may not be quite contempt,
so we have put music to uses, which, if they can be
defended at all, at least have but slight justification;
for it should be remembered that music is before all
else an *art*.

In spite of daily companionship, music remains a
mystery.   No single phrase has ever succeeded in cap-
turing all of music in one definition.   Its symbols are
easily characterized; physicists can more or less accu-
rately define its exteriors of sound and rhythm; physi-
ologists can trace its course into the human ear, and
psychologists can estimate certain reactions to it; but
once it has entered into the spirit of man and has

begun to operate in his imagination and emotions, no
definition will satisfy the diversity of its effect.   Meta-
physicians, poets, æstheticians, physicists and musicians have contributed illuminating characterizations
of it; but their definitions cover it only in part, never
embracing it in its entirety.

So, for example, Schopenhauer says, "Music is * * *
the copy of the Will itself, whose objectivity the
Ideas are."[1]

Leibnitz defines music as "exercitum arithmeticæ
occultum nescientis se numerare animi."[2]

Santayana is quoted as saying that for many people
music is "a drowsy reverie relieved by nervous thrills."[3]

Music has been characterized as "thinking in tones;"[4]
as "a presentation of emotional experience, fashioned
and controlled by an overruling intellectual power;"[5]
and in divers other ways.

Observing music's versatility and to what numbers of
situations it seems to be appropriate, we may also
remark that nowhere is music bent to a greater variety
of ends than in the service of the church.   There, indeed, it may justly be called the ecclesiastical maid-of-
all-work.   Let us name a few, at least, of the tasks to
which church music is commonly assigned.

(1) It is sometimes urged that music will put the

---

[1] *The World as Will and Idea.*   Schopenhauer.
[2] *Epistolæ, collectio Kortholti.*   Leibnitz.
[3] Quoted in *Music: An Art and a Language.*   Spalding.
[4] *La Musique, ses lois, son évolution.*   Combarieu.
[5] *Music: An Art and a Language.*   Spalding.

hearer in a frame of mind receptive to religious teaching. The use of music for this purpose is a reasonable and, under ideal conditions, a valid one. But it implies a reciprocity between preacher and music which in these times is seldom realized. Surely it would be an inspired preacher who could match the eloquence of a Lassus or a Morales; and by the same token many a parson must feel himself helpless to overcome in the pulpit the effect of the musical puerilities which emanate from the choir-loft. If a preacher depended on the music of our Protestant churches to make the congregational spirit fallow for the reception of the seeds of religious instruction, he would do much better to throw up his hands and pronounce the benediction.

(2) Perhaps the widest use of church music is for the purpose of attracting large congregations. This is not always the avowed intent of churches which advertise their music widely and which cultivate elaborate services featuring music carried on by orchestras, quartets, and highly-paid 'song-birds;' but the philosophy behind such administration is evident in the fact that success is judged by attendance and the size of the collection.[1] The music is primarily designed to please the regular congregation and those who may be attracted by the prospect of something unusual. It may be argued that in these times any means tending to stimulate church attendance is not to be neglected.

[1] It is not uncommon to hear a public appeal for generous contributions to defray the expense of 'musical' services.

Is there not, on the other hand, a strong analogy between religion and education?   Neither are novelties; the benefits of both are common knowledge; no attractions ought to be necessary to bring intelligent persons within their sphere of influence.   It is not only prejudicial to the great art of music to employ it as a decoy or a 'barker' to draw people within church doors; such use constitutes, as well, an affront to the Almighty. Worship is a privilege, not an imposition; and forcible feeding of it in any guise is revolting.

The only reason music is not more often replaced by motion pictures, dancers, and the like, is because the tradition for music in the service is of long standing, and, to a certain degree, sacro-sanct.   We need not hope, however, that where mere numbers are the chief desideratum music will not sooner or later be replaced by more startling service adjuncts.   An example of appeal through sensational methods is presented by two services lately held in a prominent Boston church, where, according to the newspaper announcement[1] were offered "a mid-summer communion service" (beach pajamas and shirt-sleeves, perhaps?); a sermon on "California Bungalow Life;" another entitled "The Greatest Robber, Gangster, and Racketeer in the World — Do you Know His Name? — His Initials are A. I.;" and climaxing these, "special marimba-xylophone selections," which, as creators of a devotional atmosphere through the employment of solo instru-

[1] *Boston Herald*, August 6, 1932.

ments of percussion hold, as far as I know, a unique place in the history of the Christian church.

It would be manifestly unfair to question the motives which lie behind such services as these. If that marimba-xylophone which may be heard nightly in hundreds of dance halls was not a mere box-office attraction, then it was a psychological blunder in very bad taste.

(3) Those who are ambitious for music to hold some primary function in devotional exercise point confidently to music's uplifting power. It will, if it be 'religious,' produce lofty emotions; it may redeem the souls of granite-hearted sinners; it may even avert burglarious intentions. Believers in this dynamic moral quality of music are ignorant of music's limitations and, above all, they persistently disregard its Janus-headed personality where emotional stimulus is concerned. Such enthusiastic well-wishers for music should remember that did it possess such remarkable gifts as they would have us believe, devout and intelligent worshippers would long ago have been moved to crimes of violence against music committees and other responsible parties.

Probably no parable uttered by our Lord has been so greatly tortured to excuse superficial thinking as that of the lost sheep; and it is again invoked to bolster up this ideal of the redemptive power of music and to circumvent the charge that certain types of music are employed mainly in the interest of creating 'popular' services. "Is it not possible," we are often asked, "that of the hundred who are drawn to church by the lure of music, one may, by its power, be brought within the fold?" And my answer is "No," for music, even the noblest music, has no power to work miracles. But even if it had, my sympathy goes out strongly to the ninety and nine who will get just what they came for, and which, it is to be hoped, they will generously pay for, departing from the church with a complete misconception of what worship means, and of what the place of music in religious exercise really is.

I have just said that music has no power to work miracles such as the creation of religious emotion and the turning of the unrighteous man from his evil way. Our attempts to make music do these things generally arise from our desire to use music as authoritatively as we use painting, sculpture, ritual and language. Thus we forget that music contains no commonly communicable *idea*. Painting or language tell the same story to everyone. The picture of a ship will not be mistaken for the portrait of a man, nor will one listening to the reading of the scriptures have conveyed to him the idea contained in the *Ode on a Grecian Urn*. Music will generate as many ideas as there are listeners and its language will be interpreted in as many ways. That a piece of instrumental music without a title 'means' a battle to one hearer, is no guarantee that it has the same definite meaning for all. To another person it may signify a shipwreck or some cosmic upheaval.

Slow, quiet music will mean the gentle motion of the sea, or wind in the trees, or the quiet conversation of lovers.[1]

Even such general characteristics as gaiety, sadness, warlikeness, or serenity are not intrinsic in any music. We call a piece martial when it employs technical means which we associate with music which has in the past been characterized as martial. But even then the case is not so simple as it seems, for suppose we hear a fanfare played on the trumpet; very likely it will suggest a call to arms or the morning awakening of a camp. It may be, on the other hand, and it sometimes is, a prelude to the *Tuba Mirum* in the Requiem.

I know that psychological opinion on this matter is not unanimous. Professor Carroll C. Pratt deals with it in his recent book, *The Meaning of Music*. Under the heading "Autonomous Music" he says:

"Whenever it is maintained that the nature or essence of music lies wholly within the borders of sound and tone, that music is *sui generis* and never serves as a sign, an expression, a symbol, an imitation, a language, or a likeness of anything except itself, when, in other words, it is held that the laws of music derive solely from the laws of hearing, then music is considered to be *autonomous*. Many æstheticians, however, and even musicians, feel a certain incompleteness in any doctrine which defines music as autonomous. Is not the content of music more than the music itself? Does not music furnish to the listener an incarnation or representation of a world of ideas and values communicated by way of music, but

---

[1] By the same token there is a great difference between listening intelligently to music and listening intelligently to language. If someone were to read you a ridiculously sentimental poem, only your sense of humor would be affected. Yet many otherwise intelligent persons are moved to sincere tears by the most outrageous musical drivel.

not identical with it? Whenever these questions receive an affirmative answer, music is regarded as heteronomous."

Somewhat later, Professor Pratt continues as follows:

"A striking illustration of the variability of meaning as contrasted with the uniformity of character revealed by music was reported at some length a number of years ago.[1] Some thirty musicians were asked to report their impressions of different compositions directly after they had been played. For some selections they were asked to note any ideas or meanings conveyed by the music; for others they were requested to describe the mood or character of the music. The complete disagreement of the reports under the first instruction was little short of ludicrous, whereas one can hardly fail to be very much impressed by the similarity of judgment given under the second instruction. The *Andante molto cantabile* from Beethoven's Piano Sonata in E, Opus 109, to cite only one example, came under the instruction to describe the general mood or atmosphere of the music. Such words and phrases as peaceful, pensive, subdued happiness, serene, placid, calm dignity, and tender happiness occurred frequently, and not a single description was given which could be considered as representing more than a slight divergence from the element which these words undoubtedly share in common."

If this test was designed to discover whether a piece of music possesses a singleness of either meaning or mood which will, within a limited area, be evident to all hearers, the choice of musicians as subjects was questionable; for some of them, surely, must have had previous acquaintance with the selections played, and all of them must, at some time or other, have heard music similar in character. Such music, if vocal, was undoubtedly set to texts whose import was 'peace,' 'tender happiness,' or other like sentiment; if instru-

---

[1] *Report on an Experimental Test of Musical Expressiveness.* **B. I. Gilman.** Published in *American Journal of Psychology*, 1892.

mental, it would have borne either a title suggestive
of these moods, or their equivalent in the familiar expression marks '*doucement*,' '*calme*,' '*con tenerezza*.'

The choice of professional or non-professional subjects is, however, beside the point. The nearest scientific approach to a solution of the problem as to whether
music is autonomous or heteronomous, would be, it
seems to me, to take twenty or so new-born babies,
insulate them from all experience of music during a
period of years, and then subject them to such a test
as is described above. In that case no associative
factors would intrude and the results might be of real
significance. I firmly believe that neither the meaning
nor the mood which a piece of music seems to possess
grows out of the music itself, but out of its association
with words or with some representative means, such
as a picture, a ritual, or a ballet; and the definiteness
with which a meaning or mood is suggested varies in
three degrees: most strongly in vocal music, less so in
program music, and least of all in absolute music.

Thus the text of Schumann's choral piece *Gypsy Life*
describes the wild existence of a roving band of gypsies.
As you listen to the singing of the words the music
seems to partake of their restless character; but play
this music to one who has never heard its text and the
piece becomes merely an animated musical selection.
In program music the persons or events delineated or
described in the literary or pictorial source of the
music are characterized in the music itself. So, in

Tchaikovsky's *Romeo and Juliet* Overture there are musical themes for the houses of Montague and Capulet and a passage descriptive of the strife between them; and whether or not you apply the proper meanings will depend first upon your knowledge of the story of Romeo and Juliet and, second, upon your knowing exactly what measures are descriptive of the different characters and events. Lacking all this, the music will be, for you, simply music. In abstract music, as I have already stated, the suggestion is variable in the highest degree.

As vocal music is quickest to create confusion as to the exact location of the *idea*, and as vocal music forms the greater part of the music of the church, this ascription of a commonly understood meaning or mood in music has worked serious damage by perpetuating the belief that music itself possesses well-defined ethical powers, and that certain types of music are 'religious.' How prone we are to say, "Such music makes me a better man. It does me more good than a sermon." Now, music apart from some idea expressed outside the music cannot have positive ethical quality. It cannot, single-handed, make one a better man, but it is a highly powerful ally to ideas of every sort, good and bad.

"It is the one art in which no human being can raise the false issue of a direct ethical influence. * * * * * Of course, all contemplation of pure beauty is ennobling, and in this sense music may have the same indirect moral bearing as a flower or a sunset or a Greek statue. But of immediate moral bearing it has none. It means nothing, it teaches nothing, it enforces no rule of life, and prescribes no system of conduct. All attempts

to make it descriptive have ended in disaster; all attempts to confine it
to mere emotional excitement have ended in degradation. Grant that
nations and individuals of imperfect musical experience have not advanced
beyond the emotional aspect: that Plato had to prohibit certain modes as
intemperate, that governments have had to prohibit certain melodies as
dangerous. In almost all such cases it will be found that the music in
question is vocal, and that more than half the stimulus is due to its words
or its topic. Considered in and by itself, the ultimate aim and purpose
of the art is to present the highest attainable degree of pure beauty and
sound."[1]

We know, for example, how potent is the influence
of music on soldiers going into battle, but the sound
of the music is not the primary cause of their rushing
against the enemy; the real issue is defense of their
land or the gaining of power or territory from some
other country. Surely we would be unwilling to
place the effect of church music in the same category
with the effect of music on animals — as when it stills
the roaring lion or quells the angry serpent; and yet
this is exactly what those religio-musical enthusiasts
are unconsciously advocating when they urge on us
the view that 'church music makes us better.' Just
as one goes to war, not because music bids him, but
because he desires some particular end, just so is one
religious, or has pious thoughts, or, to be consistent
with the layman's terminology, 'feels good,' — either
because he desires peace of mind on this earth or
because it suggests to him hope of a reward hereafter.

Music is a powerful quickener of those emotions

---

[1] *Studies in Modern Music.* Hadow.

commonly associated with religion; and in that quickening power there lies a serious danger, for we are all aware of the narrow psychological wall which separates the religious from the secular and even from the erotic.

I assume one of the predominant elements in religion to be love; but religious love, as Professor James has pointed out, "is only man's natural emotion of love directed to a religious object,"[1] adding that this is equally true of all sentiments, such as fear and awe. But these last two lie within a totally different area from that containing the sentiment of love, in so far as their sensitiveness to musical stimulation is concerned; for although music cannot evoke sentiments apart from ideas, certain emotions, such as fear and awe, lying near to the intellectual centre, are not so immediately stimulated by music, which from its very poignancy will most quickly ignite the sentiment of love, the most indefinite, versatile, and pervasive force in man. And it is this very indefiniteness which makes it, when awakened by music, a dangerous factor in religious experience.[2] If, then, there is no

---

[1] *The Varieties of Religious Experience.* William James.

[2] "Music is a two-edged sword; capable of quelling the passions, so of giving a mortal wound to virtue and religion; and therefore should always be in sober hand. . . . Quick and powerful, and penetrating the minutest parts of the body, and inmost recesses of the spirit, when employed under the banners of religion; but likewise searching, and irritating every evil thought, and intention of the heart, when debauch'd into the service of immorality and profaneness. What ought to kindle a devout affection, may blow up every evil desire into a flame, may be the fuel and incentive of vice." Sermon preached by Lavington, September 8, 1725, on *The Influence of Church Music.*

mental entity which we may call religious emotion, and hence no emotion of religious love *per se*, once the hearer's natural emotion of love has been turned toward God by idea and association, it would be well to avoid the use of music which may bring about any degree of confusion. In other words, let us not use music which contains, by association, intimations of the love element; and though the hearer may still continue to assure us that church music such as we hear to-day 'makes him a better man,' we shall fear that, in a great majority of cases, what he thinks is a higher religious ardor induced by music is, at base, only the very common element of secular love.

And those elements, apart from love, which through music find the readiest association with religion are a sense of aspiration, of exaltation, of inner peace, of detachment, of awe, and a sense of the mercy of God. I have failed even to include humility, because humility lies psychologically too near to love in the sense that both are distinctly personal emotions. Humility very easily merges into self-pity, and self-pity is akin to self-love. The idea of humility is, of course, contained in that of divine mercy, but there the thought is directed toward God and not toward the worshipper himself. Such music then, the ideal music of worship should wring from the hearer the cry "How good and how great is the *Lord God*" rather than the all too common ejaculation of the self-deceived worshipper 'How good this music makes *me* feel.'

Nor should we forget that the text, even though sacred, cannot be counted on to override the effect of music which is, by association, secular. On this point I cannot do better than to cite Grillparzer's[1] dictum, which is affirmatively quoted by Hanslick:[2]

"The essential difference between music and poetry might be brought into strong relief by showing that music primarily affects the senses and, after rousing the emotions reaches the intellect last of all. Poetry, on the other hand, first raises up an idea which, in turn, excites the emotions, while it affects the senses only as an extreme result of its highest or lowest form. They, therefore, pursue an exactly opposite course, for one spiritualizes the material, whereas the other materializes the spiritual."

Thus, if, as happens in a great proportion of our church music, the words are sacred and the music is, by association, secular, whatever religious impulse might spring from the text is destroyed by the more rapid action of the music. It is not unimportant to remember that comparatively few churches supply their congregations printed copies of the texts sung by the choir; careless pronunciation, moreover, has always been a reproach to church singers.[3] So it is that the effect of an anthem is often a purely emotional one emanating from the sound of the music. A similar

---

[1] Complete Works (Vol. IX). Grillparzer.

[2] *The Beautiful in Music.* Hanslick.

[3] "And to return to the expression of the ditty, the matter is now come to that state that though a song be never so well made and never so aptly applyed to the words, yet shall you hardly find singers to express it as it ought to be: for most of our Church men, (so they can crie louder in the quier than their followers) care for no more; whereas by the contrairie, they ought to study how to vowel and sing cleane, expressing their words with devotion and passion, whereby to draw the hearer as it were in chaines of gold by the eares to the consideration of holy things."

Plaine and Easie Introduction to Practical Musicke. Thomas Morley (1597).

situation occurs in the opera house, where, in the course of a season, thousands of persons will nightly sit, enchanted by the spectacle and the music, while not one word of the text, if it be in a foreign tongue, is intelligible to them.

One has only to consider how generally superior to their musical settings are the texts of anthems, hymns, and solos, to realize how devastating may be this emotionally instant action of music. In exactly the opposite way from which not a little of Schubert's vocal music persists in spite of the shoddy literary quality of the texts, so, much church music holds its place merely because the texts are notable or familiar in religious literature. Rarely in church music does one find such equality of excellence as was supplied by the poets and composers who adorned the great Elizabethan age of secular music. Few composers have found themselves bold enough to attempt a setting of the words "O death, where is thy sting, O grave, where is thy victory?" — words full of the most poignant associations for us all. It took no less a composer than Brahms to make even a fair musical match for this text. Composers of less distinction, however, have not hesitated to rush in where discretion should have dictated otherwise. The majestic and long-breathed passage "I am Alpha and Omega" as set by Stainer and done 'in style' by a pompous bass suggests nothing so much as the declarations of a comic opera potentate. Tons of such anthems, some of them better, some of them worse, but none of them good, are in current use only by virtue of their text and because association seems to impart to the music at least some of the nobility of idea which resides within the words.

This is, alas, true of hymns as well. The Latin hymn with its plain-song setting presents the rare phenomenon of a parity of worth between text and music. So, to a great extent, does the choral. But these types are not common in our Protestant service. In their place we have as literature a body of poetry of varying excellence, and as music, material which is largely secular. That the music does not seem secular is only due to the fact that we never consider it apart from its texts. So many of our Protestant hymn-tunes are literally chafing in bondage. If they could only get out into the world where they could be themselves, as love-songs and serenades and melodies of broken hearts; but no, someone has got them between the rigid covers of a hymnal and they never will escape from it. They must go on pretending to be what they are not and sounding more self-conscious and mildly naughty than perhaps they are, just because they know they don't really belong in the hymnal. Consider the plight of a tune like *Galilee* to the words "Jesus calls us." Here is a melody of infinite social possibility. I cannot at the moment think of a more ingratiating or insinuating bit of music. If it should once escape from the hymnal, it might even become a wrecker of homes. It is probably safer where it is, numbered and indexed, and sung by guileless Christians at the Feast of good Saint Andrew. The tragic fact is that much church music is so bad, even considered as secular music, that there is literally no place for it outside the church. Yet this is the music we term 'religious.'

Now it may be observed that I have labored euphemism in an effort to avoid the phrase 'religious music' because there is no such thing. Those who assert that all good music is religious music in the sense that it is suitable for performance in church or capable of arousing religious sentiment belong to that large class of persons who rhapsodize and sentimentalize music from indefiniteness into inaccuracy, and who disregard, or are ignorant of, the tricks association will play us. The man who said "Wagner is my religion" suffered from this very haziness of idea as to the real function of music in worship.

If music seems to be religious, it is so not because of any religious quality inherent in the music itself, but simply because of its alliance with religious texts and titles, or because it is performed in church. Many pieces originally set to secular words are given in church with the substitution of a sacred text; and because we have never heard the music sung to its secular text, but know the selections only in their church form, we are deceived into thinking that the music itself is religious. Certain of the choruses in

Händel's *The Messiah*, for example, appeared originally as love-songs for two voices: notably, "For unto us a Child is born" and "All we like sheep have gone astray." The celebrated Passion Choral, "O Sacred Head, now wounded," before its baptism into the Christian faith which involved some ironing out of irregular rhythms, was sung as a five-part madrigal to the words "My peace of mind is shattered by the charms of a tender maiden." With less reason, then, may music be termed 'religious' when its primary use is not only secular but is, as well, familiar to us in its secular state. Does the hackneyed music of "Last night I lay dreaming of thee, Love, was dreaming *etc.*" become 'religious' simply because it is frequently sung in church to the words "O eyes that are weary and hearts that are sore, look off unto Jesus and sorrow no more?"

It is clear, then, that we ought not to accord to music any inherent religiosity or to ascribe to it ethical powers. Those historians who give credit to music for the conversion of St. Augustine award to music an impossible eminence. If St. Augustine, through meditation or some other intellectual process, had not got hold of the idea that it was time for him to be a better man, all the music in the world would never have shunted him on to the track of saintliness. The memory of one's mother, or the fear of God may prevent one from committing arson or murder, but the recollection of a particularly telling performance of

"Hark, hark, my soul" by the church choir will never
serve as an effective deterrent to unrighteousness.
It is also clear that the position of music in worship
must be secondary: as an ally, a servant, or a contributor it has undoubted value; but unintelligently used,
and burdened with responsibilities which are foreign
to its substance, it may be comparatively valueless
or even downright obstructive.

(4) In one group may be gathered such superficial
uses of music as the adding of variety to the service,
the covering up of pauses, the supplying of the minister
with breathing spaces, and many others equally foot-
less, but none the less oft-proclaimed. It is only necessary to add that music is a pleasant interruption to
the main business of worship and a delightful concomitant of stained glass windows and over-stuffed pews
to round out a play-theory of the union of art and
religion.

(5) The noblest use of music under any conditions,
it seems to me, is the employment of music as a sacrifice (in the Old Testament sense, if you will), an
oblation, which on Sunday we offer in the name of
the Almighty. Now, although my reason for the
advocacy of this view is primarily idealistic, it has
a pragmatic force as well, for a review of the usually
held objects of church music which I have listed,
together with any others I may have omitted, leaves
the selection of the actual music to the widest variety
of personal opinion, circumscribed by all sorts of atti-

tudes and conditions. Even the use of music as a
preparation for teaching, a means entirely possible
psychologically if ideally administered, leaves the
choice of music an individual matter. And what is
'ideally administered?' Certainly there would be
many persons who would select for the above purpose music which others would consider out and out
bad. The indefiniteness of opinion in such a matter
is illustrated by another quotation from Professor
James Pratt:[1]

"Especially is the congregational singing of hymns productive of considerable religious feeling; while the rendering of selections by the choir at
times aids in producing the desired religious atmosphere — provided the
selections be really religious and the rendering of them sincere."

May we not properly ask what is a "really religious
selection" and what is a "sincere rendering?" Each
person will answer this question for himself, and we
shall be no nearer a standard than we ever have been.[2]
Not even professional musicians, whose judgment of the
quality of music ought to be moderately uniform, should
decide so important a matter. A theory as to the type
of music ideal for worship ought to transcend personal
judgment of any kind, and the sacrificial theory does.
Surely no man will claim the right to determine just

[1] *The Religious Consciousness.* James Bissett Pratt.
[2] Articles occasionally appear, written mostly by clergymen and laymen who
plead for a higher standard of church music. Hymns are called 'shoddy', anthems
'cheap', solos 'sensational'; then almost invariably the writer pronounces sentence
on himself by referring to "Holy, Holy, Holy" (*Nicæa*) as an ideal hymn; "I will
sing of Thy power" by Sullivan as the *ne plus ultra* in anthems; and Gounod's "O
Divine Redeemer" as the height of the desirable in solos.

what music God would prefer to have offered to Him. But music presented with the sole purpose of honoring God, and presented in His house, must bear some relation to Him in so far as music is capable of standing in that relationship. It may be said, indeed, that a very fair idea of what you think of God may be gained from the music you offer each Sunday in your church.

The element most markedly held in common by music and religion is mystery; it follows, therefore, that only that music is ideal for religious exercise which is, in its suggestion, quite apart from the world of our every-day thoughts and experiences; and if we agree that the music we are seeking must be productive of no worldly suggestion, we have certainly limited our field of choice far more than is the case at present. Although I regret that my ideal ignores both lay and professional opinion, those who will assert that for that very reason my theory is impossibly idealistic, should remember that the best products, and, indeed, the only normal products of worship are to be sought in the worshipper himself. The less he pays attention to the exterior beauty of the music, to the quality of the performance, and to the dress and personality of the singers, — the less he conceives all these to be for him, — the greater the contribution music is likely to make to his spiritual welfare. In proportion as he puts himself in the atmosphere of *worship* as opposed to the idea of *self-benefit*, just so much more readily will the whole emotional and intellectual transaction involving music, prayer, meditation, and sermon crystallize itself into a well-rounded and profitable religious experience.

Protestantism needs more submergence of personalities. Great preachers vie with popular conductors in their appeal to the public; singers and organists are advertised as though they and not God were the objects of worship; and laymen sit in judgment while the service passes before them for critical review. Just as a marked personality or a pulpit idiosyncrasy is a handicap to the sincere preacher, so music which appeals primarily by its charm of manner or of performance is church music of lessened efficiency. Viewed as a symbol, the music of the service can never be an end in itself, and rightly so. Impersonal, appropriate and significant, its imaginative power must depend neither on rhetoric nor rendition, but on the true eloquence that lies behind these.

The Material of Sacred Music

In attempting to determine the technical features which distinguish sacred from secular music, or, if you will, the music of the church from the music of the world, we must take into account at least seven factors: rhythm, melody, counterpoint, harmony, chromaticism, dissonance, and modality.[1] No one of these

---

[1] Limitations of space obviously forbid anything like a statement of all the varied applications of these musical elements to our problem. Only fundamental principles may be considered.

may be treated as independent of the others, none is intrinsically sacred or secular, but each has played a significant rôle in the identification of the two styles. The music we are seeking as the ideal is that which is farthest from secular suggestion. Such music should contain, if possible, none of the technical devices usually employed in the familiar music of the world; and it should, moreover, avoid such technical means as will tend to call attention to the music itself or to the performers.

RHYTHM

Of the elements under consideration, rhythm is the most fundamental and the most susceptible of isolation from the others. It is, moreover, a wholly characteristic and effective weapon of secular music. If, for example, you simply tap out the rhythm

you will probably not be reminded of some devotional hour; rather you will recall the endless jazz offerings and Spanish dances that pour unremittingly from the radio, for the particular rhythm cited above is common to popular music and is seldom heard in church.

The ease with which rhythm will transform into secular music a piece originally sacred and vice versa may be shown by two examples, the plain-song melody *Conditor alme siderum*, and the secular madrigal by Hassler (1564–1612), *Mein Gemüth ist mir verwirret von einer Jungfrau zart* ("My peace of mind is shattered by the charms of a tender maiden"). The plain-song, though it is here printed in notes of even length, is not, in actual performance, bound by even that rhythmic restriction; for, after the manner of all plain-song, it derives its motion from the accents of the text, and is, therefore, quite free of any 'pulse' or rhythmic regularity, being in the nature of musical speech. Despite the lack of rhythm such as is fundamental to all secular music, the essential melodic beauty of this tune was evident and the world borrowed it to add to the great store of folk-song. It appears here first in its plain-song form and, immediately beneath, as a French folk-song, transformed into secular music by the simple expedient of adding rhythm and of making one simple melodic alteration.

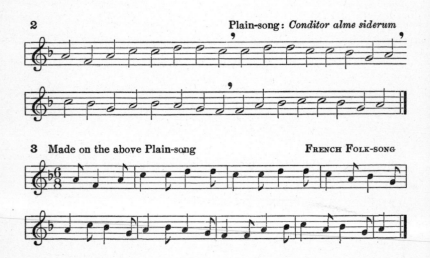

2   Plain-song: *Conditor alme siderum*

3 Made on the above Plain-song   FRENCH FOLK-SONG

The madrigal "My peace of mind is shattered"[1] offers an example of exactly the opposite method. Composed originally as a secular piece, it was converted by the musicians of seventeenth century Protestant Germany into the familiar choral "O Sacred Head, now wounded" simply by divesting it of its rhythm.

HANS LEO HASSLER
Madrigal: "My peace of mind is shattered"

Choral: "O Sacred Head, now wounded"

[1] In many of the choral illustrations only the soprano part is reproduced.

Now it may be urged in the latter case that what took place was merely the substitution of a regular $\frac{4}{4}$ metre for a preponderant metre of $\frac{6}{8}$, and this is true. But it should be remembered that any metre, when it employs for a considerable period notes of equal length, destroys the rhythmic pulse to such an extent as to nullify in most cases its secular effect. This is not necessarily true of melodies made up of equal-length notes moving with such rapidity as to give the effect of stress at the beginning of each measure, as in the following case:

LUDWIG VAN BEETHOVEN
Choral theme from Ninth Symphony
Freude, schöner Götterfunken

A comparison of illustrations 5 and 6 will show that although both melodies are made up almost entirely of notes of the same value, the slow pace at which the choral moves prohibits a regularly recurring pulse which might induce one to nod his head or to tap his foot in time with the music[1]; whereas the Beethoven melody by its relatively rapid motion establishes a regular measure pulse, which places it definitely in the field of secular music.

It is obvious, of course, that the rate of motion employed in the performance of any piece of music will affect it in divers ways; notably it may cause a radical departure from the composer's ideal as expressed in his tempo indication. A plain-song may be sung at such a speed that its melody becomes a mere blurred succession of notes and not the eloquent partner of the words to which it is set; by the same token the Dead March from *Saul* becomes a parody when taken at a rapid pace; in the same way music of quick motion may be so dragged out as to make it almost static. Within certain limits, every piece of music has a normal tempo, the serious alteration of which ends by changing the physiognomy of the music. But the speed at which a selection is performed is not the only 'temporal' condition which will affect its nature. Persistent dotting will transform an otherwise equable and dignified melody into a state of rhythmic restlessness. The melody of "Now thank we all our God," for instance, if submitted to regular dotting becomes secular in character.

[1] With the earlier composers the ideal of a flowing and elastic rhythm was more than an artistic one; it related definitely to the effect of the music; and conscientious composers of sacred music from the Middle Ages onward have felt strongly the obligation to avoid a regular pulse in their music. Modern editions of fifteenth and sixteenth century music attempt to preserve this feature by the copious tying over of notes and chords from weak beat to strong and by the initiation of motion on a weak beat.

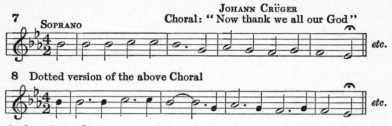

7

SOPRANO

JOHANN CRÜGER

Choral: " Now thank we all our God"

8 Dotted version of the above Choral

A further demonstration of the truth of this principle
appears in the contrast between illustrations 9 and 10,
both drawn from the anthems of Henry Purcell (1658–
1695).   The former[1] gains dignity and sacred character
by the use of undotted notes, while the latter[2] offers
full surrender to the rhythmic stimulus which arises
from the use of the dot.   Furthermore, in illustration 9
it is evident that care has been taken to preserve true
word accent by the continuation of the word "shut"
over parts of two measures; whereas in illustration 10,
sense has been sacrificed to melodic and rhythmic
vitality as shown by the treatment of the word "but"
in the third full measure.

9

HENRY PURCELL

Anthem: " Thou knowest, Lord, the secrets of our hearts"

SOPRANO

Thou knowest, Lord, the se - crets of our hearts;   Shut— not,

shut— not Thy mer - ci - ful— ears un - to   our prayers,

[1] Composed for the funeral of Queen Mary and sung, in the same year, at
Purcell's burial.

[2] Composed for the Royal Chapel under Charles II who delighted in the tuneful
and rhythmically animated French music of his day.

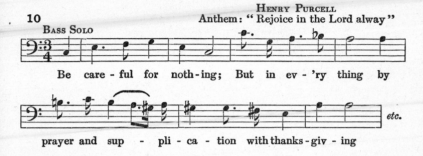

It should also be observed that the metre of the folk-song (illustration 3) and of a large part of the madrigal (illustration 4) is $\frac{6}{8}$. All forms of triple or of sextuple metre are particularly the property of secular music because in both the 'pulse' is so clearly defined. Indeed, much church music composed in triple metre and not a little of it written in moderate sextuple metre are, to all intents and purposes, waltzes. One need quote but a few examples in these lilting metres to show how inescapable is their suggestion of secularity.

12 SOPRANO

HORATIO W. PARKER
Anthem: "The Lord is my light"*

Heark-en un-to my voice, O Lord, when I cry un-to Thee; Have

mer-cy, have mer-cy, up-on me and hear, etc.

13 SOPRANO

JOHANNES BRAHMS
Part-song: "Oh, give answer" (*Liebeslieder*)

Oh, give an-swer, maid-en fair-est; Thou whose smile my

heart— en-tran-ces, Who hast slain me with thy glan-ces,

Tell me, hath— thy— heart— re-lent-ed etc.

14 SOPRANO

WALTER SPINNEY
Anthem: "Ye that stand in the house
of the Lord"

For the Lord is gra-cious, sing praise un-to His

Name, for it is love-ly; for the Lord is gra-

cious, sing praise un-to His Name, for it is love-ly, etc.

* By permission of G. Schirmer, Inc.

15. Soprano — WILLIAM F. SHERWIN, Hymn: 'Evening Praise'

Day is dy-ing in the west; Heav'n is touch-ing earth with rest. Wait and wor-ship while the night Sets her eve-ning lamps a-light Through all the sky.—

16. Soprano — HENRY W. GREATOREX, Hymn: 'Geer'

O for— a heart of calm— re-pose A-mid— the world's loud roar, A life— that like a riv- er flows A- long— a peace-ful shore.

17. Alto Solo — OLEY SPEAKS, Anthem: "In the end of the Sabbath"*

In the end—— of the Sab-bath, as it be-gan— to dawn,— came Ma-ry Mag-da-le-ne, and the oth-er Ma-ry,

* By permission of G. Schirmer, Inc.

The rigid and mechanical effect produced by the union of text and music particularly in illustrations 11 and 15 suggests a further reference to illustration 4. Choral composers of an earlier age were very sensitive to the effect of words and music in combination, especially with regard to the true accentuation of the words. It will be noted that in illustration 4 the metre is not consistent, being made up of $\frac{6}{8}$, $\frac{3}{4}$, and $\frac{2}{4}$. This results from a modern editor's attempt to reproduce the natural text accentuation which maintained before barlines were employed. Almost any attempt to reduce to regular barring the sacred or secular music of the fifteenth or sixteenth century necessarily ends in artificial or even false accentuation of words or syllables. This may be shown by an example from the madrigal "This sweet and merry month of May" by William Byrd (1538–1623). A brief passage is first presented without bars; this is succeeded by the same passage with a barring which does not destroy the correct word accent; and this, in turn, is followed by modern barring which results, in many cases, in an unnatural accent in the text. (See following illustrations: 18, 19 and 20.)

18

WILLIAM BYRD
Madrigal: "This sweet and merry
month of May"

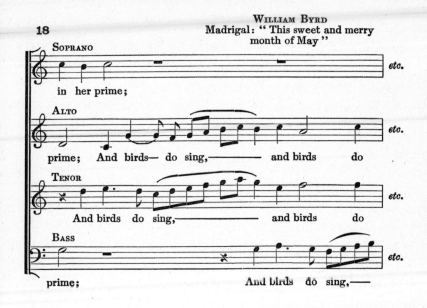

19

WILLIAM BYRD
Madrigal: "This sweet and merry
month of May"

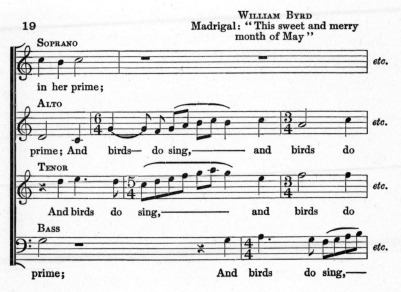

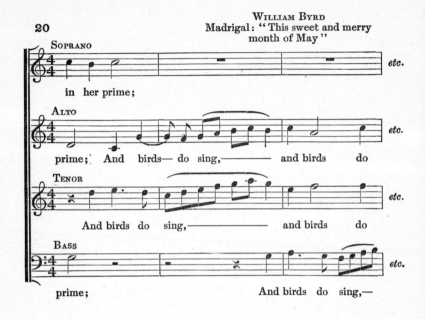

WILLIAM BYRD
Madrigal: "This sweet and merry month of May"

It is clear from the foregoing illustrations that only a system of barring such as is used in illustration **19** will insure correct word accent. A score barred in this fashion, however, presents to singers and conductors alike a very difficult problem. Editions based upon the principle demonstrated in illustration **19** have been issued, but their interest and value are mainly academic; for the performance of the older music the most practical editions are those which use irregular metres in the manner of illustration **4**. This method of preserving a true text accent is generally employed by the best modern choral composers. Two examples of this type of barring are given below.

21
SOPRANO

GUSTAV HOLST
Anthem: "How mighty are the Sabbaths"*

might - y and how deep, That the high courts of

heav - en to ev - er - last - ing keep, *etc.*

22
SOPRANO

R. VAUGHAN WILLIAMS
Whitsunday Hymn: "Come, Holy Spirit"**
(From *Three Choral Hymns*)

Lord, Thou for-giv - est our tres-pass, And call - est the folk of

ev - 'ry coun - try To the right faith and *etc.*

Sequences of any kind are questionable in sacred music because they tend to rivet attention on the music. The oft-repeated rhythmic formula was an obsession of Victorian composers whose music forms the musical backbone of so much of our Protestant usage. A passage like the following obviously constitutes a direct appeal to the listener's ear through the reiteration of the rhythmic formula found in measure one.

* *By permission of* Hawkes & Son *(Publishers)* and Miss Helen Waddell, *Author of the words, as reprinted from her book,* "Mediæval Latin Lyrics" *(published by* Constable & Co.).
** *By permission of* J. Curwen & Sons, Ltd. (Edition number: 3685).

The appropriate use of the triplet in sacred music is governed by the context and to a certain extent by the speed at which it is performed. The triplet in illustration 24 is the natural result of the composer's desire to avoid artificial word accent and to attain a logical rhythmic adjustment between words and music. In illustrations 25 and 26, however, the triplet creates merely a slight rhythmic perturbation which may, at its third or fourth appearance, set the worshipper a-jigging.

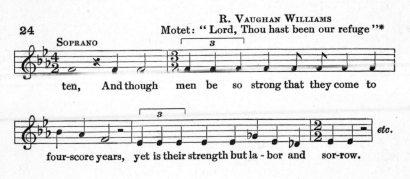

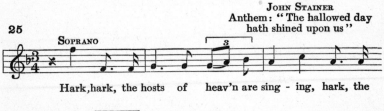

* *By permission of* J. Curwen & Sons, Ltd. (Edition number: 80592).

26

John E. West
Anthem: "The woods and every
sweet smelling tree"*

Aggressive syncopation and cross accent, the animating musical spirits of jazz, are surprisingly often met with in contemporary church music. Measures five and six of illustration 27 are representative of a rythmic method which in any of its manifestations will inevitably suggest the insinuating rhythm of the dance.

* *By permission of* Novello & Company, Ltd.

Now the part which rhythm plays in differentiating the sacred from the secular style is not a theoretical one; it proceeds out of the natural evolution of music itself, for much of the sacred part-music of the fifteenth and of the early sixteenth centuries is practically identical in its rhythmic make-up with the secular music of the same period.   But before the sixteenth century was passed, rhythm became the initial identifying mark of

* *By permission of* Oliver Ditson Company, Inc.

secular music, and for this identification three factors were largely responsible: first, the music of the folk-dance, which was, of necessity strongly rhythmed; second, the folk-song, often employed in connection with the folk-dance; and third, instrumental music, which, being for the greater part free of sacred auspices, was at liberty to make use of rhythm as it saw fit. So it was that rhythm in secular choral music became definite in pulse, often sequential in treatment, and a valuable partner to melody and harmony in the subtle characterization of text. Indeed, the skillful use of rhythm by secular composers in the Golden Age of the chanson and of the madrigal is not least among the technical achievements of that time. But it was inevitable that church music should eventually resign itself to the sway of so basic a musical element, and even before the eighteenth century, rhythm together with other primarily secular features had been very generally adopted as a part of sacred music procedure.

MELODY

Although the distinction between a *melody* and a *tune* is an arbitrary one involving the existence of a shadowy borderland inhabited by musical personalities that may be ascribed to either class, the difference between a melody and a tune is fairly clearly marked in the preponderance of cases. A melody and a tune are identical in that they are a succession of notes of

different intervals so arranged as to suggest musical
continuity. We understand a tune to be something
which is quickly apprehended and easily reproduced,
whereas a melody is a musical entity which requires
more than a superficial acquaintance for the perception of its beauty and of its full significance. Technical details such as interval or rhythm or the speed
at which the music flows have no bearing upon the
distinction between a tune and a melody; the question
is solely one of *character*. Thus, "Mighty Lak' a
Rose" and "The End of a Perfect Day" are tunes,
while the "Londonderry Air" and the 'Largo' from
Händel's *Xerxes* are melodies.   It is enough to say
that a tune being something which attracts immediate
attention to itself and which, therefore, is destructive
of contemplation, has no place in ecclesiastical music.
The following, which may be classed as tunes though
current in Protestant music, are obviously unsuitable:

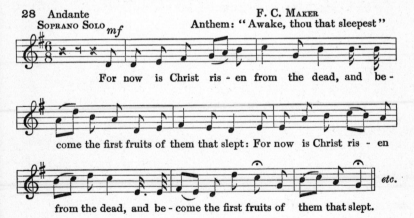

28   Andante   F. C. MAKER
Soprano Solo *mf*   Anthem: "Awake, thou that sleepest"

For now   is Christ ris - en from   the dead, and   be -

come the first fruits of them that slept: For now   is Christ ris - en

from the dead, and be - come the first fruits of   them that slept.

29

Louis Gottschalk
Hymn: 'Mercy'

God of love, that hear-est prayer, Kind-ly for thy peo - ple care,

Who on Thee a - lone de-pend; Love us, save us, to the end.

whereas the next two melodies by their remoteness
from secular association, their austerity, and their lack
of 'popular' appeal are ideally fitted for the service of
the church:

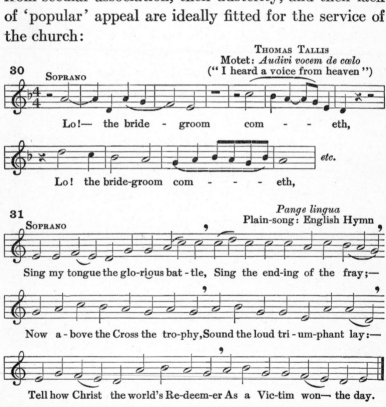

Thomas Tallis
Motet: *Audivi vocem de cœlo*
("I heard a voice from heaven")

30

Lo!— the bride - groom com — - eth,

Lo! the bride-groom com - - - eth,   *etc.*

31

Pange lingua
Plain-song: English Hymn

Sing my tongue the glo-ri̯ous bat - tle, Sing the end-ing of the fray;—

Now a - bove the Cross the tro-phy, Sound the loud tri - um-phant lay:—

Tell how Christ the world's Re-deem-er As a Vic-tim won— the day.

Apart from any arbitrary classification on the basis of tune or melody, there are certain technical features which are so frequently found in secular musical literature and which are so immediately engaging as to make them valueless in church music. Sequences, melodic fragments which repeat themselves at brief intervals, fall distinctly within this field.

32   HANS G. NAEGELI
Hymn: 'Dennis'

SOPRANO

(a)   (a)   (a)   (a)

(a)   (b)   (a)   (b)   (a)   (a)

GEORGE C. MARTIN
Anthem: " Hail, gladdening Light "*

33

ALTO   SOPRANO

The lights of eve-ning round us shine,—   The

TENOR

lights of eve - ning round us shine,—   The

BASS

lights of eve - ning round us shine,—   The

lights of eve - ning round us shine,—   etc.

* *By permission of* The H. W. Gray Company.

In general it may be said that diminished and, to a less extent, augmented intervals should be avoided in church composition because they figure so prominently in 'expressive' music. It is also true that such intervals, because they imply resolution, tend to focus attention on the course pursued by the melody, thereby making the musical interest paramount. A table of the more commonly used diminished and augmented intervals with resolution is given below.

Surrender on the part of the composer to the temptation to write church music which is sensuously effective, and the love of the singer for vocal ostentation have furnished two unremitting problems throughout the history of the church. The former is well illustrated by humming passages and wordless melodies on the syllables 'oo' and 'ah.' In the Middle Ages the singer dominated the course of church music to the extent that his vocal behavior was an open scandal; and it was only because of the fact that the secular and sacred styles had practically merged that the vocal excesses of church singers in the eighteenth century were not subject to equal condemnation. The blame for all this, however, must be shared by the composer who offered in the past and who still is offering to church singers the means of gratifying their desire for self-glorification. Even in congregational hymns, among them *Twilight* ("Now the day is over") and *St. Gertrude* ("Onward, Christian Soldiers") may be found naïve and amusing examples of licence in the form of the brass band or 'oom-pah' bass, which, aside from their musical emptiness are nothing more than a mild indulgence in vocal fun. From such elementary uses the church singer's prerogative runs the whole gamut of musical showdom. There is melodic ornamentation, for instance, such as is shown in illustrations 35 and 36.

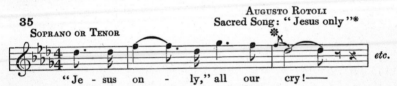

35

There are high notes which are clearly introduced for the display of vocal virtuosity and which bear no relation to the meaning of the text.

36

* *By permission of* The H. W. Gray Company.

Similarly there are low notes which offer proof that the bass singer either has or hasn't them.

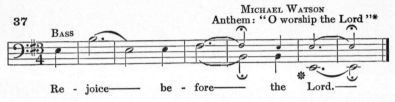

There are wide intervals which serve as dramatic occasion.

Up to about the seventeenth century there was a prevailing equality of interest between the voices or 'parts' of choral music; but with the rise of opera, of Italian vocal virtuosity, of instrumental technique, and of harmony as the controlling factor in music, the upper part (soprano) began to assume elaborate and even florid proportions with a corresponding falling off of interest in the other voices. By the time of Haydn (1732–1809) and Mozart (1756–1791) florid melody in church music was abundant in all the voice parts. A comparison of illustrations 30 and 41 with illustrations 39 and 40 will show how far the personal and display-ful element in melody had penetrated the fabric of church music in the eighteenth century.

By permission of G. Schirmer, Inc.

39 Soprano

Franz Josef Haydn
Kyrie from 'Third Mass'

Chri - ste e - lei - - - - son, *etc.*

40 Bass

William Boyce
Anthem: "The heavens declare
the glory of God"*

The heav'ns—— de - clare—— the glo - - - ry, the

glo - - - - - ry, the glo - ry of God, *etc.*

41 Soprano

Giovanni Pierluigi da Palestrina
Kyrie from 'Mass of Pope Marcellus'

Chri - ste, Chri-ste, e - lei - son, e - lei - son, *etc.*

Chri - ste e - lei - son

COUNTERPOINT

Counterpoint, or music in which all the voices are
melodies, is the earliest form of part music, and is
best illustrated by choral works of the fifteenth and
sixteenth centuries or by almost any choral or organ
composition of J. S. Bach. The purest vocal counterpoint belongs to the periods before music was affected
by harmony. Counterpoint progresses horizontally,

* *By permission of* The Oxford University Press.

harmony vertically; the former is the ideal church anthem style in that it is essentially impersonal, implying the equal coöperation of all voices instead of the exploitation of one at the expense of the others. It is, moreover, undramatic, since its full effect is almost never felt at any given second due to the constantly shifting melodic emphasis and the rhythmic diversity of the music.

The following examples show the difference in character and method between harmony (illustration 42) and counterpoint (illustration 43).

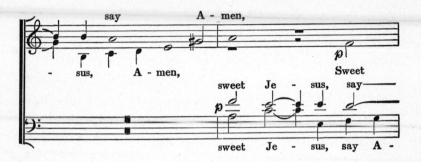

Harmony

Harmony is, in one sense, an evolution from counterpoint. Toward the end of the fifteenth century, church music had become so involved in the simultaneous use of a number of texts set to counterpoint of amazing complexity that the singer's words were practically unintelligible. Against this abuse there came a reaction on the part of composers, notably Josquin Després (1450–1521), resulting in a more consistent use of 'familiar style,' which was, in effect, simple harmony. But familiar style preserved at least the essence of part-equality and it perpetuated the church tradition against pronounced rhythm. Thus it happens that some of the most beautiful and valid church music is cast in an amazingly simple form, far easier of performance than the great body of music now in use. Observe the purity of the following passage in familiar style:

44   SOPRANO AND ALTO

LUDOVICO TOMMASO DA VITTORIA
From *The Reproaches*

Po - pu - le me - us,   quid fe - ci ti - - bi? Aut

TENOR AND BASS

Re-spon - de mi - hi.

in quo con - tri sta - vi - te? Re-spon - de   mi - hi.
Re-spon - de mi - - hi.
Re-spon - de   mi - hi.

Quite different was the need which brought about the development of harmony near the beginning of the seventeenth century, for then the world was seeking some means of making personal, dramatic situa-

tions musically significant. Counterpoint, though it
had been employed by both sacred and secular composers throughout the sixteenth century was not sufficiently graphic nor instantaneous in its effect to
intensify dramatic occasions; moreover many voices,
moving in counterpoint, cannot fittingly characterize
individual feeling. Religious factors, such as devotion, contemplation, and aspiration may be suitably
expressed vicariously through counterpoint; but love,
hate, jealousy, ambition, pain and the like are essentially personal and require one voice and a sharp accompanying musical characterization to make them
articulate.[1] So there came into use a kind of melody
which gradually grew in expressiveness, and this melody was accompanied by simple chords (harmony).

Now harmony, like rhythm, is primarily a weapon
of the secular composer, though it became eventually
the musical ideal of the Reformed church. There,
however, it was intended by its simplicity and rhythmic
directness to support congregational song. It was inevitable that the Reformed church should emphasize
congregational participation in music, and it is the good
fortune of that church that the choral has never become involved with the emasculated harmony which
has infected our modern Protestant hymnody. To say
that hymns and chorals are of equal value because

---

[1] One of the many notable psychological misfits in opera is the scene in Saint-
Saëns's *Samson and Delilah* in which the Hebrews lament their evil state in
terms of an academic fugue.

both employ harmony and simple rhythm is to ignore the fact that there is a vast difference between the melody, harmony, and rhythm of "Now the day is over" and those of "A mighty fortress is our God." The former is a texture of commonplaces and blatant secularities; the other, especially in the simpler harmonizations of Bach, is a noble work. There are, of course, good hymns, but few, alas, are current in our churches.[1] Ecclesiastical harmony should be as nearly as possible triadic, that is, made up of chords in their simplest and most familiar grouping. Seventh, ninth, eleventh, and other dissonant chords, either in root position or inverted, require resolution, and, except as they occur in the countrapuntal course of a composition, they are subject to the objection which may be raised against all dissonances which involve real discord.[2] A table containing a few triads and dissonant chords is given.

Used in harmony, dissonant chords often have a distinctly emotional significance, especially when certain

---

[1] We should remember that counterpoint is exclusively 'choir' music, whereas harmony may be either for the choir or the congregation.

[2] The implications of dissonance in church music are dealt with on pages 133–138.

of their factors are chromatically altered, a fact which the Romantic composers were not slow to perceive. Even the all too familiar dominant seventh is often an enervating presence.[1] Observe how the texture of the following phrase is strengthened and made less "expressive" by the substitution of a simple triad for the dominant seventh.

Old Saxon Melody
Arranged by HENRY CAREY
Hymn: 'America'

46

SOPRANO AND ALTO

From ev - 'ry moun-tain side Let free-dom ring! Let free-dom ring!

TENOR AND BASS

There is in addition to familiar style a kind of harmony which, without being contrapuntal in its employment of an extensive individual rhythmic life for each voice, yet preserves melodic interest in all the parts. This harmony also avoids the characteristic rhythmic pulse of secular music. Such musical material is ideal for choir use:

[1] The dominant seventh is never more deadly in church music than when it appears successively in different keys. The ogling effect of such a use is inescapable. For a good example of a bad practice the reader is referred to the hymn-tune *Galilee*.

47

16th Century Melody
Harmonized by MICHAEL PRAETORIUS

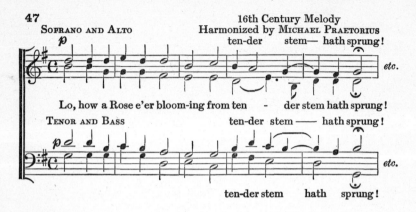

48

HANS LEO HASSLER
Cantate Domino

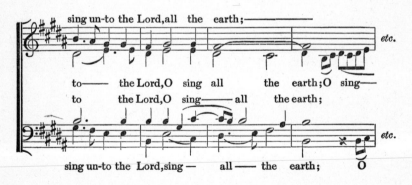

As choral material for the service, harmony in any form cannot vie with counterpoint. But the former has three valuable uses: first, when used in composition to create relief from the prevailing counterpoint; second, to supply music for choirs which in numbers and in skill are unequal to the demands of music which is technically taxing; and third, to furnish congregational singing with a solid background of chords.

CHROMATICISM

Chromatics are generally used in church music for three purposes: for modulation; to heighten the expressiveness of a melody; and to add color to the music. The first of these is the only use legitimate in church music. as the others greatly enhance the emotional dynamic of the music. It is true that certain sixteenth and seventeenth century composers of church music employed chromatics here and there in the alteration of a single note of the melody or chord with telling effect, but any extended chromaticism such as became current in the seventeenth century and has continued to our own day is bound to produce an effect of restlessness, of emotional stimulus and of secular suggestion.

Particularly in melody is their employment pernicious; the following melodies, one of them secular, the other sacred, will show how chromaticism affects the quality of a melody:

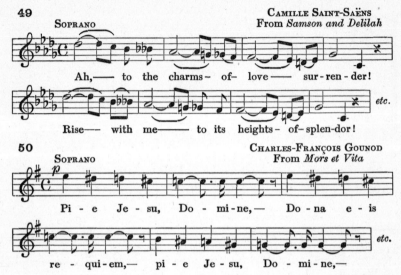

These are, of course, cases of extreme chromaticism, but any chromatics in the melody or harmony of church music except as they occur in simple and widely spaced modulations should be discreet. An example of a less offensive but none the less unsound chromatic church melody is:

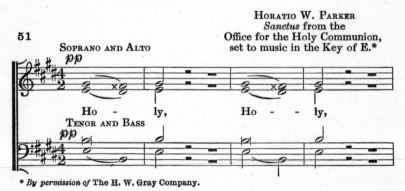

* *By permission of* The H. W. Gray Company.

In harmony the free use of chromatics establishes at once a secular atmosphere. Such progressions as

represent harmonic formulæ common to everyone's musical experience and are the groundwork of secular chromaticism. Augmented harmony, represented by (a), (b), and (c), and familiarly known as 'barber shop' harmony, appeared in church music as early as the seventeenth century, used by composers whose chief interest was opera and the field of secular music in general. Since that time the use of this particular type of chromatic harmony for the purpose of 'prettying up' church music has been constant.

The following are offered to show how inevitably uniform in result is chromatic use in any style and, therefore, how unfit for ecclesiastical music:

53 Soprano and Alto

JOSEF RHEINBERGER
"Night Song"*

And gent - ly breez - es are sigh - ing,

And gent - ly breez - es are sigh - ing, The

Tenor and Bass

lake seems to throb in glad pain;—— spite

54 Soprano and Alto

GEORGE C. MARTIN
Anthem: "Ho! everyone that thirsteth"

cresc.

Hear, and your soul shall live,

Tenor and Bass   cresc.

soul shall

dim.   rall.

your soul, your soul— shall— live.

dim.   rall.

* By permission of G. Schirmer, Inc.

Illustration 53, a fragment of a secular part-song, is typical in its chromaticism of the Romantic secular choral style of the nineteenth century; illustration 54, though sacred music, employs the same chromatic method. While we may be shocked at the bald adaptation to sacred ends of an eminently secular means in its lower manifestations, such a procedure is preferable to the bromidic chromatic harmony employed at measures 3 and 7 in illustration 55, where the moonlight-with-young-lovers-in-the-foreground effect is unmistakable. The effect just referred to is the triad on the sixth degree of the major mode with lowered root and fifth. The flatted sixth of the major scale has long ranked so high in the musical vocabulary of the composer of sentimental ballads and popular songs and has become so hackneyed by endless repetition that it is almost never used in this day save as a means of parodying sentimentality. The dance hall's fling at it is familiar to us through the following brief coda often appended to dances of a lively character.

56

One is more and more impressed by the wisdom displayed by the guardians of the church music of old.

Even in the Middle Ages the use of chromatics (then called *'musica ficta'* or *'falsa'*) was forbidden except for the purpose of rectifying the disagreeable effect of the augmented fourth (called 'the Devil in music'). Through the sixteenth century, chromatics were used by most church composers with taste and discretion, but men like Marenzio (1560?–1599), Gesualdo (1560?–1614), Weelkes (*circa* 1575–1623), and, in particular, Monteverdi (1568?–1643?), masters in the adroit use of chromatics as expressive agents in secular music, left a beguiling heritage which church composers, even to our own time, have all too fully drawn upon.

DISSONANCE

In this analysis of the material of sacred music I have used the term 'dissonance' as meaning a musical effect requiring 'resolution,' *i.e.* completion. At this point, however, I want it to assume its other meaning, namely that of a discord in the popular sense.

Discord in music is, first of all, the result of a perfectly natural desire for contrast. If music progressed with exclusive concordance, it would be indeed a tame matter. Just as an earthly existence unrelieved by stress or difficulty would soon make weaklings of us, or as consistently sweet food without some relief would quickly sicken us, so music must have its compensating effects of discord. But my parallels are drawn from life, and it is music apart from the life of the world that we are seeking. Therefore, dissonance, if it is to be a factor in church music, must be regulated with care. But music, regardless of the uses to which it is put, is, first of all, an *art*, so it would be foolish autocratically to exclude any elements from it which are essential to its existence.

The inappropriateness in church music of sharp dissonance was fully realized by church composers of the sixteenth century. Palestrina, who more than any other composer succeeded in establishing an air of complete aloofness from the world, confined himself in his church music to consonance and near consonance; his employment of dissonance in the sense of discordance was generally designed to heighten the effect of the text. Thus in *The Reproaches* at the word "Egypt" ("Did I not bring thee out of the land of Egypt?") he used a dissonance which is in marked contrast to the rest of the musical material. That Palestrina was aware of the secular power of dissonance is proved by his telling use of it in his madrigals. His contemporaries, like Vittoria and G. M. Nanino, went even farther in their sacred music in the use of dissonance than did Palestrina in his secular style; and while they wrote beautiful church music which is far more colorful and emotional than Palestrina's, they are in so far less convincing as church composers than he.

Palestrina's name has been so often invoked where purity of style is under consideration that it seems

redundant to mention it here; but when church music
consists of a hodge-podge of styles made up of whatever happens to tickle the ears of thousands of American laymen, parsons, and organists, it will do no harm
again to say that among church composers of part-
music Palestrina stands above all others in his ability
to exclude worldly suggestion and even human emotion from his music.   So absorbed is he in the act of
devotion that his music often seems almost motion-
less.   Particularly in the quieter motets, one imagines
the composer, head bent, hands clasped before him,
deep in meditation.   Byrd's church music is supreme
in another field; for if Palestrina's music is often no
more than *attitude*, Byrd's music is *gesture:* the quiet,
inevitable gesture of one who must at times lift his eyes
and stretch out his hands.   The following passages,
though brief, will suggest this difference:

WILLIAM BYRD
Motet: *Ave verum Corpus*

Palestrina and Byrd stand, then, as two exponents
of the ideal of sacred choral music. Other composers
have translated emotion into music in varying degrees,
but the farther they have departed from Palestrina's
simple triadic, non-chromatic, non-dissonant, almost
anti-rhythmic style, with its melodies sometimes quoted
from and never far removed in character from plain-
song, the nearer they have approached the suggestion
of the secular. And as dissonance is a sure vehicle of
emotion, so only the most sparing and controlled use of

it is permissible in sacred music. Never should it be used for its own sake, that is, as a means of creating a musical effect, but only where it serves to heighten the text, or where to avoid it would damage the integrity of the contrapuntal flow.

Three examples of discord are given below: illustration 59 presents a purely 'musical' and therefore an indefensible use; the discord in illustration 60 results from the text, and the dissonant effect in illustration 61 arises from the natural progress of the counterpoint:

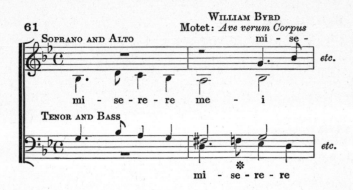

MODALITY

It is difficult to say whether rhythm or modality constitutes the most distinct line of cleavage between the sacred and the secular styles. The modes are the scales upon which music is constructed, and as such they play an important rôle in characterizing the music of which they are the basic substance. The church music with which we are familiar is built upon two modes which are also the modes of practically all current secular music, namely, the major and the minor. The music of the Middle Ages was richer than ours in that it possessed fourteen modes of which six were eventually either discarded or absorbed in the first eight by a process known as 'reduction.' The eight modes with their finals and dominants indicated by black notes are here given:

62

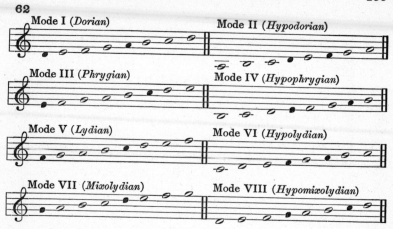

These modes, as well as the other six, were also the material of secular music, notably of folk-song, and one of them, the Ionian, was so popular in profane music that the Church, calling it 'modus lascivus,' forbade its use in sacred practice.

Now this Ionian mode is identical with our major scale, and one reason for its popularity, a reason that applies equally to our major mode, was the presence of a half-step between the last two degrees. For some reason the ear has apparently always sought relief from the austerity engendered by the interval of a whole tone moving upward to end a melody, and it was inevitable that the church musicians of the Middle Ages, even like their modern brothers, should have been unable to resist the lure of the secular, with the result that we have much plain-song which, though not called Ionian, is interval for interval in that mode. Plain-song written in modes which involve the upward

progression of a whole tone at the close are obviously
more churchly in feeling than are those plain-songs
composed in the major mode which includes the interval of a semi-tone between the seventh and eighth
degrees. It is only necessary to reproduce a Gregorian
melody ending with a whole tone, and then to transform a part of that melody into the major by means of
chromatics, to prove how the sacerdotal quality of the
original is dissipated by such alteration. The presence of harmony, superfluous though it is and alien to
plain-song, serves to heighten the secular effect of the
altered version.

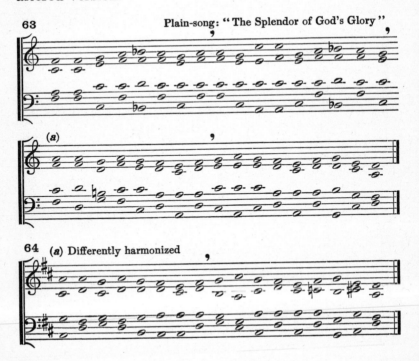

63   Plain-song: " The Splendor of God's Glory "

(a)

64 (a) Differently harmonized

The older modal system, then, unfamiliar in substance, is ideal for the service of the church. Some modern composers of church music have realized this, as the profoundly sacred quality of the next illustrations will show:

65   A. Tchelishchev
Cherubim-Song

66

CHARLES WOOD
Gloria in Excelsis from
' Short Communion Service '

SOPRANO AND ALTO

O Lord–God, Lamb of——God, Son– of the Fa - ther.

TENOR AND BASS
O Lord God,

O Lord God,

"As to the question of scale it may be true that in time the more austere modes of church music lost the sympathy of those impregnated with the major scale of daily life; though it is a little difficult to see why, if this is the case, men have always been able to use conversational English for daily life without losing sense of the greater beauty of the more austere English of the Bible. However that may be, there are quite certainly in modern composition signs that composers now realize the rich opportunities presented to them by these very modes which for so long lay discarded and unworked."[1]

PARTICULAR CONSIDERATIONS

Difficult of appraisal on the basis of technical analysis is that body of church music which may be said to occupy a stylistic no man's land: music made up of empty formulæ; music which is no more than innocuous rhetoric; easy to sing, easy to learn, and difficult to forget. The music of Mendelssohn (1809–1847), both sacred and secular, was the great prototype of this style, but Mendelssohn's genius, technical skill, and taste made some, though by no means all, of his sacred choral writing suitable for church use. Scores of composers,

[1] *Elizabethan Church Music.* Published in *Church Music Society* — Occasional Papers, No. 3.

particularly in the Victorian era, succumbed to the
lure of his beguiling facility and produced a universe
of uninspired, technically correct and hopelessly commonplace music, which the American Protestant Atlas
has borne and is bearing smugly upon its shoulders.
This music is not offensively secular; it is merely an
aggregation of notes arranged with words; as anthem
or hymn it serves to fill out a period of the service; it
does not shock us by its pronounced secularity any
more than it projects us into a world far different from
our own.   It is, at best, a deplorably pale sacrifice.
Three quotations will suffice to suggest the thousand
anthems and hymns which are vain repetitions of
idealess musical clichés.

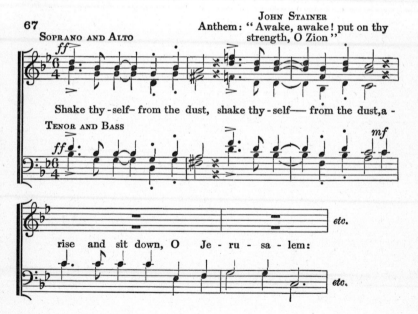

68
JOHN E. WEST
Anthem: "The eternal God is thy refuge"*

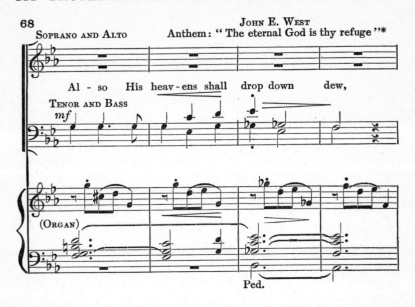

* *By permission of* The H. W. Gray Company.

69

JOSEPH BARNBY

Anthem: "O Lord, how manifold are Thy works"

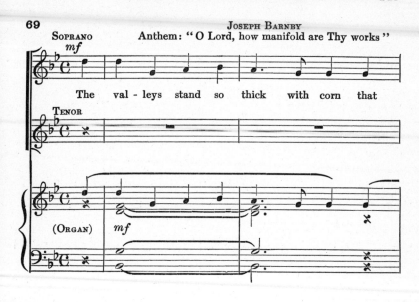

The val - leys stand so thick with corn that

they laugh and sing, they laugh and sing, they laugh and

There are composers other than Mendelssohn who make difficult the exact definition of a standard, but for quite another reason. These men are not numerous, because they represent a degree of genius expressed in such individual and eloquent terms that not only is imitation of them by other composers all but impossible, but the classification of their music as belonging to sacred or secular style is often difficult as well. Such a composer is J. S. Bach (1685–1750), a great amount of whose choral music set to sacred words would not withstand such analysis as I have lately suggested.[1] Yet the altitude at which so much of his

---

[1] This does not, of course, include the superb and simple choral settings of this composer.

music is conceived seems to place it above criticism based upon any arbitrary technical requirement. It would be difficult to discover secular suggestion in the following measures although they represent a violation of several principles laid down in the foregoing analytical material:

70   Johann Sebastian Bach

Soprano and Alto   From *The Passion, according to St. Matthew*

Little of the sacred music of Josef Haydn (1732–1809) is suitable for either the Protestant or Catholic services. It was not until late in life that, under the spell of Händel's 'grand' style, he composed choruses like "The heavens are telling" which, in their fervor and simplicity entitle them to inclusion at church festival occasions. But it is Händel (1685–1759) above all, who by the sheer majesty of his musical eloquence can almost make us forget the fundamentally secular quality of his sequences and rhythms. A good illustration of Händel in one of his regal moments is the following:

71

Now, I am led to make two observations which seem to me important for a proper understanding of this section devoted to the technique of church music. First, if one were to apply literally the critical yardstick of my technical analysis to church music, a measurable quantity of music set to sacred words would go by the board. That is inevitable and perhaps desirable. On the other hand, a standard fixed by any inflexible critical method may well be too mechanical to be just. In literature it often happens that words or phrases taken by themselves assume a significance quite apart from the context that surrounds them; so in church music a single technical detail to which exception might be taken, unless it be persistent or patently destructive of the style to which it is supposed to minister, may be offset by a wealth of pertinent material. Second, if I appear to be inviting an elastic application of my ideal by my willingness to include context as a factor in this problem and by my acceptance of exceptional musical personalities like Bach and Händel, let me say with the utmost definiteness that I would rather withdraw entirely these qualifications than have them serve as an excuse for the misinterpretation or misapplication of the principles I have laid down.

Music to Fit the Ideal

Five classes of music are in use in Protestant churches:

1. (a) Music familiar to everyone and originally set

to secular texts which have been displaced by sacred ones. Such are, for example, "Ring out the sweet message that Jesus will save" to the music of "The Bells of Saint Mary's;" "Sweet the moments rich in blessing" to the music of Donizetti's sextet from *Lucia di Lammermoor;* and "The holy hour, so sweet to me" to the music of Nevin's *The Rosary.* It is surely unnecessary to comment on the employment of such selections as these under the guise of 'church' music.

(b) Instrumental music designed for performance under secular circumstances and now converted to the Church's use: "Lord, we pray in mercy lead us" to a melody from Sibelius's *Finlandia;* "Land of hope and glory" to the music of Elgar's *Pomp and Circumstance March;* and "Goin' Home" fitted to a part of Dvořák's *From the New World* Symphony. These selections in their proper instrumental setting are so frequently heard in concert halls as to make indefensible their inclusion in the service.

(c) Secular music which through unfamiliarity or technical change has ceased to have any secular significance. No better example of this type may be offered than the choral "O Sacred Head, now wounded," mentioned on page 97. The important requirement to be made of music of this type is that it shall in its original state be unfamiliar to everyone; for church music is not a sacrifice of the few or of the many, but of all.

2. Music which, regardless of its origin, is secular in its technical make-up: such music, except under the special conditions named below in section 4, is invariably inadmissible.

3. Music so negative and commonplace that it would be rejected as art under respectable conditions either sacred or secular, and which, as church music, occupies merely a negative position. An examination of Protestant service lists discloses the use of an appalling amount of this material. It is preferable, of course, to music of secular import, but it ought to be replaced by music of real calibre.

4. Music drawn from the works of outstanding geniuses the nobility of whose language occasionally transcends questions of idiom or style. These composers may, perhaps, be counted on the fingers of one hand, and their names do not bulk large in Protestant musical practice. This is due not so much to the alleged difficulty of the music, as to the almost instinctive reaction against it as music unlikely to please the congregation.

5. Music, which, by its unfamiliarity and its absence of secular suggestion is the primary property of the Church. This is, above all others, the music best fitted to the ideals enunciated in this book.

To this music belongs, as the highest example, (1) Plain-song. This is easily the simplest and, incidentally, the least expensive medium for worship music. Plain-song is always sung in unison and may be supported by a type of instrumental accompaniment suited to enhance the beauty and quality of the melody. Any accompaniment to plain-song, however, is an intrusion and ought, wherever possible, to be omitted. (2) The music of the sixteenth century contrapuntists, much of which (particularly the selections mostly in familiar style) is so easy of performance that an average amateur chorus, diligent in practice and competently trained, can perform it.   (3) The Reformation choral, either in its simple settings for congregational use or in the slightly more complicated settings of Bach, which are suitable for choir use.   (4) The anthems of the Reformation and seventeenth century Protestant composers who based their church styles on the simplicity and sincerity of the choral.   (5) The work of some seventeenth century English composers, notably Orlando Gibbons, Tomkins, and Henry Purcell. (6) Some of the motets of seventeenth century continental composers, particularly those whose departure from the Palestrina tradition was not extensive, or who preserved the spirit of the choral in their writing. (7) Certain pieces of notable eighteenth century geniuses.   (8) A comparatively small amount of nineteenth century music, mostly Mendelssohn and occasional works of his few inspired disciples.   (9) Modern Russian church music which, in spite of its variance from the technique of the sixteenth century, has yet recreated in no little degree the spirit of the sacred music of that age.

For the organ there is a considerable amount of excellent music written by the school which preceded Bach, and there is the great body of organ literature composed by Bach himself. Händel, Brahms, Franck, and certain of the moderns — notably those who employ modality — have contributed organ music worthy of acceptance on the highest critical grounds. It is not necessary to enlarge this catalogue. Organ music, like hymn or choir music, is susceptible of reference to a definite standard, and by that standard it should be judged.

Now I feel that I ought to anticipate one individualistic and thoughtless objection to the music I have cited, an objection which is often met and which is raised particularly against the music of the sixteenth century, namely its 'lugubriousness.' In the first place, church music is not to be listened to with reference to its ability to cheer us up. That is, perhaps, the preacher's function. But more than that, the protested music, if it is received in the proper spirit and not criticised as something we expect to please us or to make us smile or to produce some purely subjective effect upon us, *will* cheer us up, in the *sacred* if not in the *profane* sense; for this music literally breathes assurance, comfort, and hope, and these, I take it, are cheerful elements in the religious if not in the secular meaning of the word. The preacher who said "Church music should make us uncomfortable," was, perhaps, overemphatic, but I suspect he had been irked once too often by such irrelevant criticism as I have cited.

I assume also that a question will be raised as to the æsthetic quality of the music which accompanies the ideal.   If this music is to be a sacrifice, must it not be the *best* music; must it not, in its field, be the equal of Brahms's and Beethoven's symphonies and of Mozart's chamber music?   The answer is obviously "yes," yet I shall not attempt to justify this music on the grounds of my own taste, for my ideal and the music are a unit. If you accept the ideal you must accept the music also, because it is the only music that fits the ideal; if the music is bad, then the ideal is bad, because inferior music can never be a perfect sacrifice; if you reject the ideal on the ground that the oblative idea is distasteful and my psychological and technical predicates false, then the question of the quality of the music automatically ceases to bear any relation to the problem. Question the worth of this music if you will but let the music itself be its own apologist.

Now it is not true that the music I am advocating for use in the modern church will necessarily fulfill the demands of the future; while the ideal is naturally fixed, the music may be variable, for its validity depends upon its unfamiliarity and its dissociation from secular suggestion.   Should it become customary to dance to Plain-song, to march to Palestrina, or to eat to the accompaniment of Bach's chorals; in other words, should the world adopt as its own the characteristic music of the sanctuary, then indeed would we be obliged to seek for the consummation of our ideal quite a different music from that which I have advocated.

The worship music of the future, however, need not concern us. It is enough to know that all our present needs are met by music at once accessible, provided with English text, inexpensive, and much of it not difficult of performance. But, alas, how little is the voice of that music heard in American churches; how slight the opportunity for it to exert its persuasiveness. And for this the blame must be placed squarely upon the musical profession. Many choir-masters, it is true, have little or no acquaintance with the church classics; others are limited in various ways to the extent that the music is incomprehensible to them and ungrateful in sound; but it is with those who have a real understanding and love for it that it is difficult to be patient, for they will not even attempt to give it a hearing; they exhaust sophistry in their evasions — their choirs couldn't sing it, choir-masters would lose their positions if they attempted it, and last and inevitably, congregations would go to some other church where they could hear the music they like to hear. Before offering such objections as these, every educated choir-master ought to ask himself five questions: —

1. Do I look upon my church position as a professional contract or as a privilege to service?

2. Do I regard church music from one of the many utilitarian points of view generally held concerning it, or have I some positive ideal?

3. Am I persuaded that to use any but the highest type of service music is destructive of my self-respect?

4. Am I acquainted with the literature of church music, or am I content with what publishers send me, with what other choir-masters use, or with what I have always used?

5. Have I made an honest effort to induce the clergy and laity of the church I serve to give a hearing to my convictions in this matter and an opportunity to argue the validity of those convictions through the witness of great music?

In asking this last question in particular, I am not proposing that it shall be answered by an aggressive campaign on behalf of better church music which will arouse active hostility. Nothing would be more undesirable. But before accepting as inevitable the automatic rejection of this music by congregations, it ought to be remembered that for months we allowed a national policy of shilly-shallying and side-stepping to earn us the scorn of nations who were fighting our battles; that the draft, perhaps the most drastic legislation in our history, was received with comparative calm; that the undreamed-of threat of national prohibition became a fact; that we are profiteered and racketeered; that we are overtaxed and underfed; and that our patience with the inane eloquence of American legislators causes the rest of the world to marvel at our forbearance. Yet we have endured all this, and we do still endure it, like lambs. I find it difficult to believe, then, that if on Sunday we choose to substitute a good anthem for a poor one, the congregation of the First Baptist or St. Peter's Episcopal will depart riotously in numbers, perhaps destroying as they go.

Choirs and Instruments

Church music is carried on by means of voices and instruments. The voices group themselves into the mixed quartet, the male quartet, the men's chorus, the solo, duet and trio, the boy choir, and the mixed choir. The organ is the instrumental constant in the church service, though other instruments are used from time to time. Always eager to avail itself of musical means which the world finds attractive, the church has of late years cultivated a type of organ which exploits the percussion devices of the orchestra, such as the celesta, which suggests fairy bells, the harp, and the chimes. These are the particular property of theatre organs and their sound is a familiar element in moving-picture experience; therefore, they have no place in a church organ. The best organ literature, moreover, ignores them, and their use in such music is foreign if not actually hostile to the composer's intent. As all other instruments thrive primarily in secular surroundings and bear the inescapable suggestion of the concert hall, their employment in church, except for semi-secular occasions, such as state celebrations, is unjustifiable.

But the choir is the central problem in the practice of church music. In this age of specialization, of the professionalizing of the arts, of taking your beauty and your religion vicariously, the choir is all-important. Because of the inability or unwillingness of the congregation to bear its part in musical worship, upon the choir falls the major portion of this service.

THE MIXED QUARTET

Among the organizations used to furnish Sunday music, easily the most popular is the professional mixed quartet. For those to whom the sensuous effect of church music is of prime importance, this group has one immediate advantage: no matter what type of music is sung, it generally has lavished upon it some degree of vocal skill, for the members of a mixed quartet are usually selected for their individual ability as singers. They may not and often do not have any interest in the church which employs them or in the service to which they minister, save to hold their positions and draw their pay. They are literally hired minstrels. Their professional skill makes them popular with many organists because a brief rehearsal Saturday afternoon or Sunday morning before the service suffices as preparation.

There are several features which make the mixed quartet conspicuously unsuitable. First, they emphasize the personal element which is so destructive to the

mood of worship.[1]   Each of the four voices is characteristic and easily identified and generally capable of
emotional variety, and the solo is its natural expression.   Moreover, only a comparatively small amount of
the best church music is possible of performance by a
quartet; much of it is in more than four parts, and all
of it represents an expanse of idea and expression that
is impossible of realization by a group of four voices.
The reduction of a great canvas to a miniature is an
artistic abomination, and the quartet is capable of
reproducing only miniatures.   This results in the dis-
tortion of music really intended for a large group, or
in the performance of anthems composed especially for
this medium by modern composers in the modern
idiom.   The mixed quartet is to the chorus what the
string-quartet is to the orchestra.   Imagine, if you
will, a string-quartet performing the first movement of
Beethoven's *Fifth Symphony*, or a mixed quartet singing the *Hallelujah Chorus*.   As a conveyance of the
best church music ideals the mixed quartet is fundamentally inadequate.

The Male Quartet and Men's Chorus

The flair for the male quartet is passing; its present
vogue is limited to the melancholy field of funerals.
There was a time, however, when this group was as
regular a feature of the 'evening service' as was the

[1] It is significant that while Brahms composed secular music for the mixed quartet, all his sacred music in parts is for chorus.

glass chandelier in Victorian drawing rooms. It is significant that comparatively few of the really great composers have written for the male quartet, and these have generally confined themselves to the field of secular expression. Men's voices, due to the small range which lies between the top note of the first tenor and the lowest note of the second bass, and to the essential uniformity in color among the four parts, offer small opportunity for extended or varied musical expression. Counterpoint, except in its rhythmic aspects, is largely wasted on this medium, and the cloying richness of the vocal texture soon fatigues the ear. Such music lends itself almost instinctively to what the layman calls 'close harmony:' that is, harmony which, sliding along familiar and well-lubricated channels of chromaticism, provokes the palpitating listener to long ecstatic sighs. It is doubtful whether any other music can vie with the typical so-called 'male quartet' in its purely physical effect upon one class of listeners. I wish that the youth of this generation, who tend to take their religion easily, could have witnessed the emotional power exercised by the male quartet in full cry. Congregations used to, and, I suppose in some quarters still do react to its offerings very much as cats do to catnip; the narrow confines of the pew alone prevented a worshipper under the spell of "Some Sweet Day" from rolling over on his back and purring aloud.

Music for men's voices, and particularly for the male quartet, is, indeed, music of the sentimentalist. Perhaps that is why these gentlemen figure so largely in funeral services where they regale the mourners with tear-compelling 'vacant-chair' and 'we-shall-miss-him' pieces. For those who luxuriate in sorrow and who believe that to have one's emotions wrung to the squeaking point is of the first importance at a funeral, the male quartet is the perfect medium. Why we should in so poignant an hour summon four individuals, whose only interest in us may be calculated in dollars and cents, to supply an artificial stimulus to the tear ducts of us and our friends, it is difficult to understand.

Most of the objections which apply to the male quartet are true of the men's chorus as well: namely, limited range, monotonous color, over-opulent vocal texture, and emotional potentiality, all of these leading to a literature restricted in amount, variety and quality. The men's chorus is, of course, superior to the male quartet in that by its added numbers it avoids the intensely individual quality bestowed on the music by only four voices. Moreover, the men's chorus, due again to its numbers, is capable of performing church music of real substance. This music, except for some Italian editions of church pieces susceptible of performance by 'equal voices' (that is, by a chorus of men's or women's voices) is to be found mostly in arrangements of music originally composed for mixed chorus. Such arrangements are undesirable, as they pervert the composer's intent and furnish only a counterfeit of the original, but where men's choruses are in use in churches, these arrangements are better than the specially composed material offered in most publisher's catalogues. Men's choruses survive particularly in college chapels where a combination of tradition and the anti-co-educational complex prevents the use of women's voices. For the shorter and less formal daily services a men's chorus may be most convenient, but a college chapel is, after all, a church, and nothing should prevent the establishment of the highest musical standard there.

The Solo

If a quartet is undesirable because, through its limited numbers, it calls attention to individuals and so destroys the mood of worship, so three, two, and one singer respectively are proportionally undesirable. But by inverse ratio the music increasingly improves. There are many beautiful sacred solos, but the best of them are drawn from oratorios which are primarily dramatic works. The church solo is economical and saving of rehearsal, but these reasons certainly cannot weight against its obvious inappropriateness.

The Boy Choir

The boy choir might have been dealt with earlier in this book under 'Tradition,' for to tradition is almost entirely due its survival; sentimentality, too, plays a large part in its retention. As against the one occasion when the layman comments on the musical excellence of a boy choir, he will a hundred times remark on their angelic appearance in cassock and cotta, on the fact that it is good discipline for boys to belong to such an organization and that through choir membership they become interested in the church. But a choir is, first of all, a musical organization. Neither charm of appearance nor disciplinary value is of importance in determining its validity. Among the many objections to the boy choir which may justly be raised are the following:

1. Due to the lack of discipline among American children, much time which could be profitably spent in rehearsing an adult chorus must be wasted on extra-musical matters.

2. Our climate in many parts of the country is unfriendly to the singing voice and really good American boys' voices are not numerous.

3. Boys learn their music slowly, forget it easily, and are readily upset in performance by any untoward incident.

4. At a point, where, through a developed voice and some length of experience boys become valued choir members, their voices change and they must be released from service.

5. Boy altos of real calibre and sufficient musicianship to hold their part are the exception, and they are generally replaced by men altos whose tone is quite different from that of the boy soprano, so that real tonal unity is impossible.

6. As boys' voices are not strong enough to lead congregational singing, a very important part of their function is lost.

This type of choir, however, is alone acceptable to those laymen who believe that women should be excluded from choir participation on the ground that their voices generate the wrong kind of emotion — an argument, if I may say so, which is characteristically masculine and which deserves to be answered on its own plane. If women's voices produce the wrong kind of emotion in men, then do not men's voices produce the wrong kind of emotion in women? And have not women, as well as men, souls to be saved? Now the layman may be nearer right than he appears to be, but the real answer to his argument is, first, that we select the wrong kind of women's voices; second, that we choose the wrong kind of music for them to sing; and third, that we cause it to be sung in the wrong way.

It will readily be admitted that well-trained boys' voices produce a sexless and impersonal tone which is ideal for the performance of the best church music; but it is also true that girls of late high school and college age sing a much better tone and one quite as impersonal. If parishes which struggle Laocoön-like in the toils of the boy-choir problem would replace boys' voices with the voices of young women the gain in every way would be immeasurable; for girls' voices possess all, and more, of the virtues and none of the vices of the boys' voices, and their use does away with the multiple and varied difficulties which beset the maintenance of a boy choir.

There is another objection to the boy choir which it seems impossible to circumvent: namely, its artificiality, both personal and artistic. If the members of the choir are co-ministers with the clergy, it is difficult to see as ministers thirty or forty boys trying not to talk or wiggle, sitting under the glittering eye of a choir-master and two or three mentors, and waiting until church is over to be boys again and not little dressed-up imitations. Moreover, to those who believe that a ministry should at least be intelligent, the boy choir is most unacceptable in that it has no real comprehension of what it sings — either words or music — and fortunately so, for you do not expect a child to recite the Bible or Shakespeare with a full understanding of their meaning, nor to play Beethoven's sonatas with comprehension of their musical significance. Why, then, should you expect him to deliver intelligently (which decidedly does not mean with personal emotion) the great texts and music of the church? If he seems to do so, it is the more painful and only adds to the already considerable sum of his unnaturalness and makes him the innocent contributor of artificiality and pretense.

THE MIXED CHOIR

By far the most effective choral organization is the mixed choir. The musical literature written for it is extensive and embraces a vast quantity of comparatively easy material suitable for the conveyance of the ideals expressed in this book. As its membership is presumably made up of mature and intelligent singers, matters both of discipline and of performance need not be considered.

The most desirable type of church chorus is the volunteer choir; but where necessary, a small weekly fee paid to twenty or thirty singers would total much less in the course of the year than the amount paid to many professional church quartets. For such a chorus trained voices are not necessary; some natural vocal ability supported by a willingness to work and devotion to the ideal are the requirements. But interest among the members will be sustained with difficulty unless two factors are present: first, the finest church music and, second, a conductor who believes thoroughly in the validity of that music and who has sufficient skill and understanding to present it properly to his choir and to produce the best performance of it of which his singers are capable. All this is of the greatest importance, because no amateur organization can sing good music well with less than two rehearsals a week; and if the music be inferior and the conductor unskilful or insincere, the chorus will quickly lose its interest.

In past generations a chorus containing many members below the age of thirty was looked upon as of doubtful dependability; men and women between the ages of thirty and fifty, seasoned in choral experience and vocally endowed, were sought as choir singers. Perhaps the present generation's greatest contribution to musical understanding is the exploding of the two fallacies that a chorus composed of really young voices cannot sing great and even difficult music, and that good choral singing depends upon the excellence of the individual voice. Young choruses, composed for the greater part of untrained singers, perform their part in the service with a vocal and mental elasticity and a degree of spirit impossible to older singers. Frank scepticism and even ridicule were the order of the day when college glee clubs began to undertake the classics; now these organizations sing with authority such works as Brahms's *Requiem*, Bach's *B-minor Mass*, Beethoven's *Missa Solemnis*, as well as modern works which try musicianship and vocal skill. Even more striking and significant is the performance of sixteenth century madrigals, of motets of the great church composers, and of modern part-songs by present day High School and Junior High School choruses. The best choruses and choirs are made up of singers from eighteen to thirty years of age, and except in the rarest of cases, the voices of singers over thirty-five years of age are a doubtful asset to any choir.

The chorus choir, particularly of the volunteer class,

has been a very general failure in this country, and the causes of this may be easily listed: first, the absence of a will to sing which results from a school experience devoted to technical drill and inferior music; second, the desire of the congregation for beautiful voices before all else and an expressive and sometimes sensational type of performance of which the quartet is the supreme example; third, the selection of poor music; and fourth, choir-masters who either feared to attempt an elevation of the standard, or who were content with the traditional order.   Young people who are at present enjoying in enlightened schools and colleges the opportunity of singing the best music will desire to continue that experience in both secular and sacred choral activity.   But to hold their interest, good music and good leadership will be necessary.

Conclusion

The purpose of this book is mainly to offer a concrete program of Protestant Church music which shall serve as a basis for discussion.   The author hopes for more than mere acquiescence or disagreement; he hopes to provoke serious thought upon a crucial matter, thought which shall lead toward conviction of some sort; for without reasoned and deliberate opinion no intelligent action will result, and modern American Protestant Church music bears melancholy testimony to the superficial mental effort expended on it in the past.

This book, then, is not written in a missionary spirit or in anticipation of some frenzied activity in behalf of immediate betterment; least of all does the author desire a 'League for Better Anthems' or an 'Alliance for the Extermination of the Bass Solo.' The forces which may bring change are a part of time, one almost fears, of eternity.

That there is no prospect of immediate improvement need not dismay us. If, after centuries of organized and authoritative effort, the Roman Church leaves much to be desired in its treatment of music, surely the Protestant branches, younger, and as yet disorganized, are far from ready for any fundamental or lasting reform. One has but to consider the superb musical heritage of the Roman Church, a body of music unequalled in purity of style and eloquent of everything for which the Roman faith stands, officially sanctioned for use in Catholic Churches, yet neglected to a great extent by the very congregations for which it was composed. Or one needs but pass in review the fulminations of the clergy and the edicts of many Popes, which in the long history of the church have been aimed at musical abuses in the service, to observe how fruitless has been all effort there to preserve an ideal of church music excellence. If, then, the church of Rome, secure in an authority which is absolute in its decrees, has chosen to depart from its highest traditions, how shall we expect the Protestant Church, divided in doctrine and subject to no central authority, to unite in a movement to improve church music conditions?

Of one thing I am confident, and I dare believe that all who have read this book will agree with me: namely, that a thorough church music renaissance will come only through the *education of future generations,* an education which will be not only musical, but which will stimulate in every child a sensitiveness to beauty of every sort; such an education as would result in a cultivated clergy, an enlightened laity, and a conscientious and thoroughly equipped musical ministry.

In the meantime, there is opportunity for individual effort. Courage, patience, self-sacrifice, faith and a high determination may not of themselves take us far upon the road to betterment; but without them, and failing a firmly grounded belief in the right of beauty on the highest plane to a place in worship, there can be no initial movement toward the realization of a better standard of service music in our churches.

And if the effort be difficult and beset with discouragement, shall we, therefore, abandon it? Not by any means. What clergyman has not been tempted either to avoid the whole question or to ask of his organist the type of music he felt sure would please the congregation and which would at the same time afford him the comfortable sense of conducting his services in the security of the familiar and the traditional? What layman has not yielded to the unthinking acceptance of the music he knew and liked without asking himself whether in the solemn hour of devotion he ought not to demand the *best* regardless of all considerations utilitarian or personal? What choir-master among us has not coveted the praise and the repute that is the reward of spectacular performance and of a choice of music calculated above all things to insure congregational approbation? Though they were said long ago and of something quite different, the words "Neither shall I offer burnt offerings to the Lord my God of that which doth cost me nothing" should apply equally well to our administration of church music: for to lift men, even for a moment, above earthly association by the power and the beauty of sound is at once a great service and a perfect sacrifice.

APPENDIX

The following four brief lists have been compiled without especial reference to the variety or the chronological range of their contents. They are merely intended to be representative of the type of church music which conforms in general to the ideals set forth in this book.

I. Hymns

Ein' Feste Burg ("A mighty fortress is our God")

O Mensch, schau Jesum Christum an ("O Holy City seen of John")

Das neugeborne Kindelein ("Where cross the crowded ways of life")

Yattendon ("Lead, kindly Light, amid the encircling gloom")

L'Omnipotent ("Father, to us Thy children humbly kneeling")

Was frag ich nach der Welt ("Let all the world in every corner sing")

Nun danket alle Gott ("Now thank we all our God")

Sine Nomine ("For all the saints who from their labors rest")

O Haupt voll Blut und Wunden ("O Sacred Head, now wounded")

Donne Secours ("O Strength and Stay upholding all creation")

Christe Fons Jugis ("Lord of our life and God of our salvation")

Christe Mutter stund mit Schmerzen ("It is finished! Man of Sorrows")

Wach auf, mein Herz ("My soul, awake and render")

O wir armen Sünder ("In the hour of trial")

Von Himmel hoch ("Now that the daylight fills the sky")

II. Anthems

O Lord, increase my faith......................GIBBONS
Let my prayer come up into Thy presence.........PURCELL
Thou knowest, Lord, the secrets of our hearts.....PURCELL
To Thee alone be glory (From 'Cantata 41').........BACH
O Gladsome Light..........................KASTALSKY
Then round about the starry throne..............HÄNDEL
Jesu, Word of God Incarnate (*Ave verum*).........MOZART
Credo......................................GRETCHANINOV
O Lord, my God (*O bone Jesu*)................PALESTRINA
Grant us to do with zeal.........................BACH
Let Thy merciful ears, O Lord..................WEELKES
Call to remembrance, O Lord....................FARRANT
The souls of the righteous (*Justorum animæ*).........BYRD
Hail, hail, True Body (*Ave verum*)..................BYRD
Cherubim Song...........................RACHMANINOV
O sing unto the Lord (*Cantate Domino*)..........HASSLER

III. Organ Selections

Psalm XIX................................MARCELLO
Choral Prelude: "Ach Herr, mich armen Sünder"...KUHNAU
Three Chorals.............................FRANCK
Prelude in G................................PURCELL
Choral Preludes: "O Mensch, bewein' dein Sünde gross"
         "Vater unser in Himmelreich"
         "In dulci jubilo"
         "Wir glauben all' an einen Gott, Schöpfer"
         "Ich ruf' zu dir, Herr Jesu Christ" ....BACH
Eleven Choral Preludes........................BRAHMS
Symphonie Romane (*first movement*)...............WIDOR
Ten Pieces..................................GIBBONS
Choral Improvisations: "Wachet auf, ruft uns die Stimme"
       "Dir, dir, Jehova, will ich singen"
                       KARG-ELERT

Choral: "Von Himmel kam der Engel Schar" ...BUTTSTEDT
Benedictus...................................COUPERIN

IV. Junior Choir Selections (*Unison and Two-part*)

Prepare thyself, Zion.............................BACH
Prayer.....................................BEETHOVEN
How beautiful are the feet......................HÄNDEL
My heart ever faithful..........................BACH
Come, together let us sing.......................BACH
Christmas Song................................HOLST
Let us now praise famous men........VAUGHAN WILLIAMS
The heavens proclaim Him..................BEETHOVEN
Tantum ergo ("Therefore we before Him bending").BEOBIDE
Up, up! my heart, with gladness ....BACH

INDEX